THE KNOTTING & BRAIDING BIBLE

The Complete Guide to Creative Knotting including Kumihimo, Macramé and Plaiting

Dorothy Wood

D&C
David and Charles

CONTENTS

Braiding

INTRODUCTION

Knotting and braiding are skills that have been around for centuries, and interest in the way they can be used in craft applications has grown in recent years. Although quite different, knots and braids are interlinked in many ways: they use cords or threads as a base, they are constructed with simple moves that can be combined to create quite complex structures, and they may benefit from being embellished with beads.

I've been fascinated by knotting and braiding for many years: I remember watching my brother make his own toggle for his scout neckerchief and loved learning to tie knots myself in the Girl Guides, and at art college I used knotting techniques such as macramé as a medium for some exciting wall hangings. In my first bible title, *The Beader's Bible*, I began to explore macramé as a jewellery-making technique, so I am delighted to be able to build on these skills, researching and learning new techniques that I could share with you in this new book. I've chosen an eclectic mix of knots and braids that are particularly suited to making jewellery, accessories and home-style applications and I hope that you will become just as enthusiastic as I am about trying out different techniques such as plaiting, Kumihimo and macramé.

It is easier than ever to source materials for knotting and braiding – gorgeous cords and threads in wonderful colours, interesting findings and fastenings, and easy-to-use equipment such as the disks and plates for Kumihimo. Whether you start at the beginning or dip in and out, you'll find each technique clearly explained with step-by-step instructions illustrated with hundreds of photographs and diagrams. There are a dozen fabulous projects using the knots and braids in innovative ways, described in step-by-step detail with 'you will need' requirements (see Projects), and as an added bonus, there are lots of additional mini ideas included throughout so that you can learn a technique and make something straight away!

ESSENTIAL EQUIPMENT

If you are already a keen beader or craft person, much of the equipment and many of the materials listed are things that you will generally have in your workbox. You don't need to get everything at once as you can always improvise, but for best results it is better to use a similar material or the equipment and tools listed.

Cords and Threads

Knotting and braiding techniques can be worked in a huge variety of different threads and cords. The choices available are reviewed in this section, and for information about the most popular cords and threads used for Kumihimo see Cords and Threads for Kumihimo.

Choosing cords

Once you have learnt a technique, do experiment with different materials as you will be surprised at the results. Knots can lose definition when worked with a soft cord such as satin rattail or embroidery cottons, and the shape can be much more distinct when a stiffer cord such as Superlon™, wax cotton, or round leather thong is used. Before you start, consider how you want the finished item to look and choose your cord or thread accordingly. Remember that each of these cords are available in a range of thicknesses and can be worked singly or in multiple bundles.

The cords and threads that have been used throughout the book for the step-by-step photographs are not the only cord or thread suitable for each technique and certainly not necessarily the best option, but they have been chosen because they show the knotting and braiding as clearly as possible.

Cord guide

This sample board of cords shows at a glance some of the cords that are suitable for knotting and braiding and gives you a quick guide to the range of thicknesses available in the different cords.

Satin cord (rattail)

This silky cord has a high sheen and is available in a range of thicknesses: bugtail is 1mm thick, mousetail 1.5mm thick, and rattail is 2mm thick, however, in practice all tend to be called rattail now. The cord is quite soft so it doesn't support the shape of knots very well and it isn't very hard-wearing.

Chinese knotting cord

This nylon braided cord holds its round shape when it is worked. Currently available in 0.4–3mm, the thicker cords are particularly suitable for knotting techniques. Finer cords are popular for macramé and Shamballa-style bead bracelets. Look online for the widest colour ranges, but you will find that the choice of colour for the thicker cords is not as extensive.

Wax cotton cord

Wax cotton cord is suitable for a range of techniques. Look out for thicker 3mm cord, which works particularly well for individual knots and knotted braids as it holds its shape well. Thinner wax cotton is ideal for macramé and easy to string with beads. They are available in natural shades and a range of colours, many of which follow current fashion trends.

> If wax cotton cord softens from overuse or you want to reuse a length, pull through under a medium hot iron to smooth kinks and restore the finish.

Superlon™

Superlon™ (often abbreviated to S-lon™) is an industrial strength twisted nylon cord originally used for upholstery. It is available in 0.5mm and 0.9mm widths and both are suitable for micro macramé and other knotting techniques where you want a fine braid or finish. These cords are perfect for adding beads into your knotting or braiding and can be mixed with thicker cords for a change of texture. Both sizes are available in a range of neutrals and pretty contemporary colours.

Paracord

This chunky cord is commonly available in two thicknesses: paracord 550 (4mm) has seven strands down the centre and paracord 450 (2mm) has four centre strands. Paracord is perfect for making bracelets and other accessories from single knots and single width knotted braid, and as it is quite bulky, it is

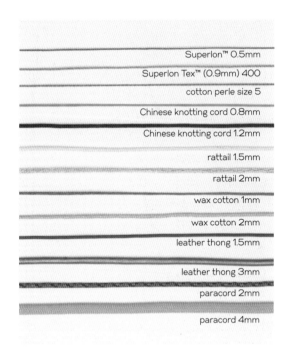

popular for men's jewellery. The cord is available in a wide range of solid bright and dark colours as well as in many multicoloured patterns.

Leather thong

Round leather thong makes a good distinct knot as it is a firm cord. It is available in a range of thicknesses from around 0.5mm up to 6mm. The thinner cords are good for tying knots and the thicker cords more suitable for use as a core to tie the knots around. Leather thong is available in natural shades and a wide range of colours. Pearlescent finishes, usually in pale pastels, are particularly attractive as are the different thicknesses of snakeskin effect cords.

Faux suede

This flat microfibre cord looks like real leather suede, but is much more pliable than the real thing and gives a completely different look to knots or knotted braids. It is generally 3mm wide and available in a range of colours.

Embroidery threads

Stranded cotton and cotton perlé are just two readily available threads that can be used for knotting, plaiting and braiding. Embroidery threads are soft and won't hold the shape of a knot firmly but they look good when combined with stiffer cords. The colour range is much greater than for other cords, so exciting colour schemes are possible. While embroidery threads are usually matte, you can use metallic embroidery threads to add a touch of sparkle.

Wire

Wire is not often used for knotting techniques because it is difficult to tie the wire without it getting kinked, although some knots created with more of a wrapping technique, such as the pipa knot, can be worked in wire. Wire, especially bundles of finer wire, can be used successfully for any Kumihimo braid, and it is also used for some finishing techniques for knotting and braiding (see Finishing Techniques for Knotting and Finishing Techniques for Braiding). For more information about using wire for Kumihimo see Cords and Threads for Kumihimo.

Choosing wire

Wire used for knotting and braiding techniques needs to resist breaking even when it is bent back and forwards several times. Most craft wires have a copper core that makes them suitable but you can experiment with all sorts of wire. The main jewellery wires are reviewed here but remember that two or more thinner wires are easier to manipulate than one thick wire.

Copper wires

As it is an inexpensive material, copper wire is suitable for experimenting with for both knotting and braiding techniques. Most craft wires have a copper core with the colours enamelled and the metallic finishes plated. You don't often get a choice of hardness with copper craft wires but I have found that those sold specially for crochet or knitting are softer and less prone to snap. Remember, also, that thinner wires are easier to manipulate than thicker wires.

Silver wire

Although expensive, silver wire will elevate any jewellery project to another level. It is available in a range of thicknesses, with soft, half-hard and hard being the most common, as well as different cross sections such as round, square, rectangular and D-shaped. Choose a soft condition wire as it is easier to work – you'll find that even half-hard wire is more difficult to work.

Coated wires

It is worth experimenting with coated wires, either paper, plastic or wrapped with fine thread, as these are less prone to kink and you can get surprising results.

Aluminium wire

Aluminium wire can be thicker than copper core wires as it is much softer, but use nylon-jaw pliers wire to prevent the wire getting damaged.

Twisting a double length of thinner wire together using a pencil or small hand drill (cord winder) makes the wire less prone to kink so making it easier to manipulate into a knot or braid than the equivalent thicker wire.

Wire gauges

Wires are available in a range of thicknesses or gauges and sold by millimetre, standard wire gauge (swg) or American wire gauge (awg). Several strands of a 0.315mm (30 swg) wire is good for Kumihimo and a 0.6mm (24swg) ideal for finishing jewellery with a plain or wrapped loop (see General Techniques). You'll notice that the thinner the wire, the higher the swg or awg.

mm	swg	awg		mm	swg	awg
0.2	36	32		0.7	22	21
0.25	33	30		0.8	21	20
0.315	30	28		0.9	20	19
0.4	27	26		1.00	19	18
0.5	25	24		1.2	18	16
0.6	24	22		1.5	16	14

Beads

Beads can be added to all the knotting and braiding techniques in a variety of different ways, either during braiding or knotting or afterwards. For more information see Beaded Knotted Braids and Beaded Kumihimo Braids.

Choosing beads

Beads come in all sorts of colours, finishes, sizes and shapes, but for knotting and braiding the size of hole is paramount so the beads can be easily strung onto the cord. It is a good idea to take a sample of cord with you when you go bead shopping.

Seed beads

This is a generic term used to describe the tiny glass beads used primarily for bead stitching and stringing. Basic seed beads (rocailles) are doughnut shaped, and the most common sizes are 15 to 3 (1–5.5mm) with 15 (1mm) being the smallest; cylinder-shaped beads, also known as delicas or magnificas, have larger holes and the double delicas can be strung onto 1mm cord. Look out too for unusual textures like the triangle, hex or charlotte beads, or for different shapes such as papillon (or peanut) beads and magatamas (drop beads).

Large beads

There are so many different beads that can be used in braiding techniques from simple wood beads to exquisite pearls and crystals, and the choice is yours. Bead hole size need not necessarily restrict you as some beads have surprisingly large holes, such as the Swarovski Mini-bead range, where even the 6mm beads fit onto 1mm cord. Pandora-style beads have very large holes and will fit over 6mm cord.

Focal beads

These extra large beads are often used as a focal point for a piece of jewellery. You can suspend pendant beads onto braids using a bail, or attach cords to large ring beads to work macramé or other knotting techniques. Remember too that large beads can be attached between two lengths of braid that have been finished with end caps.

Findings

Findings are all the little pieces, generally made from metal, that are used to make and finish items of jewellery or other accessories. Many of the findings are used to cover the raw ends of cords or braids and it is important to choose the correct size and shape. Keep a good selection of findings in your workbox so that you can create and finish different pieces.

Finishing ends

These findings are used to finish the ends of braids and knotted cords. There are more and more styles being manufactured year on year and most are available in a range of metallic finishes. For best results, match the measurement of the internal dimensions of the finishing ends to the cord or braid. Some finishing ends incorporate a fastening but if this is not the case, see Jewellery Fastenings for your options.

Cord ends

Used to finish single cords, some styles have lugs that you secure over the cord with pliers, others are tubular and are either secured with glue or with an integral crimp ring.

Spring ends

One of the older styles of finding, these can be cylindrical or cone shaped. Tuck the cord or braid inside the wire coil, then use pliers to squeeze only the end ring to secure.

End cones

These cone or bell-shaped findings can either have a hole at the top or be finished with a loop. For best results use jewellery glue to secure the braid into both styles (see General Techniques).

End caps

End caps are cylindrical, square or rectangular versions of end cones, and they too either have a hole at the top or are ready-finished with a ring or loop. For best results use jewellery glue to secure the braid into both styles, and you will find information on how to add a plain or wrapped loop in General Techniques.

Ribbon crimps

As the name suggests, these are designed to cover the raw end of ribbon, but they can be used to finish flat braids or cord. To prevent it from getting damaged, use nylon-jaw pliers to close the ribbon crimp over the braid.

Basic jewellery findings

These are the basic components of many styles of jewellery. All findings are now available in a range of different metallic finishes including antique, so choose the most suitable colour to match or contrast with your braid.

Jump rings

Round or oval, these rings can be opened and closed with flat-nose pliers, and they are used to connect items or attach other findings or fastenings. The smaller rings, 4–6mm, are less likely to pull open than larger rings.

Split rings

These are made from a hard metal coil (like a key ring), so they are more secure than a jump ring. Use split-ring pliers to prise them open to attach them to other findings.

Headpins

These straight wire findings are used to make bead dangles with a plain or wrapped loop (see General Techniques). They have a plain or decorative end to stop beads falling off and come in different lengths. Soft wire headpins are easier to manipulate.

Crimps

Generally used with bead stringing wire, these tiny doughnut shapes or tubes are secured with crimp pliers or can simply be flattened with flat-nose pliers. They are used on single wire to space beads or on doubled wire to secure to a jump ring or fastening.

Eyepins

These are straight pieces of wire of different lengths with a round loop at one end. They are used mainly to make bead links or to create a loop with an end cap attached at the end of braid.

Calottes

Sometimes called bead tips, these little domed findings are used to neatly attach fastenings when stringing beads. The basic calotte has a notch in one dome; for extra security choose a clamshell calotte that has the hole in the hinge.

Jewellery fastenings

There are lots of different findings used to finish pieces of jewellery such as necklaces, bracelets, earrings and rings. I've chosen a few styles of fastenings suitable for using with knotting and braiding. Some of the fastenings are end caps (see Finishing Ends) with a magnetic fastening incorporated in the design; otherwise, choose a style that matches the end cap and complements the braid in colour and weight.

Toggle fastening

This two-part fastening has a T-bar and ring; turn the T-bar on its side to slot in or out of the ring. Choose a more decorative style as a design feature.

Magnetic fastenings

These neat fastenings have a very strong magnet incorporated in the design. They are perfect for finishing necklaces and bracelets. If you are worried about the clasp pulling apart, add a safety chain.

Trigger clasp

This inexpensive fastening with a spring closure is suitable for finishing both bracelets and necklaces. Available styles include the lobster claw and bolt ring.

Plastic clasps

These plastic clasps are specially designed for knotting techniques such as macramé as they have a bar end to attach the cords to. The clasps are available in a range of sizes and a variety of bright colours.

Multi-strand clasps

These are available in a range of styles. The box shape is suitable for necklaces and the slider fastening is ideal for macramé and other cuff-style bracelets. Choose the number of rings on each side to suit the project.

Tools

Aside from Kumihimo, knotting and braiding techniques require little in the way of specialist equipment, indeed it is likely that most beaders or crafters will have any tools needed in their workbox already, so you should be able to get going straight away. Refer to Kumihimo: Equipment and Materials for information about what you need to get started with Kumihimo.

Jewellery tools

A basic set of three tools is needed to turn braids or knotting into jewellery. It is always worth buying good-quality, fine tools as these will help you to finish things in a neat and professional way, but avoid mini-tools as these will make your hands sore if used for long periods.

Wire cutters (1)

I usually spend a little more on wire cutters as these make life much easier. Choose side cutters, or preferably flush cutters, that cut a straight end on wire or headpins. Remember to cut with the flat side of the cutters towards the work or facing away from the tail.

Round-nose pliers (2)

These pliers are used to make loops with wire or headpins. The jaws are cone-shaped so you can vary the size of the loops by working near the top of the jaws for small loops and near the bottom for larger loops. To make loops the same size, always work the same distance down; I generally work about 6mm (¼in) from the top of the pliers.

Flat-nose pliers (3)

These are used for manipulating wire and headpins, or for opening and closing jump rings. Always look for fairly smooth surfaces on the inside of the jaws – pliers from the local hardware store are unsuitable as apart from being too big, they will probably have deep serrations for grip, which will damage the wire. Blunt-end pliers are the workhorse tool but snipe-nose (chain-nose) pliers with tapered jaws allow you to get in closer.

Specialist tools

Although not essential, this kit will help you to finish jewellery in a professional manner, so consider making the investment if you can.

Bent-nose pliers

These are essentially snipe-nose pliers with a right-angle bend in the jaws, allowing you to get into awkward positions and to hold wire or headpins at a more comfortable angle as required.

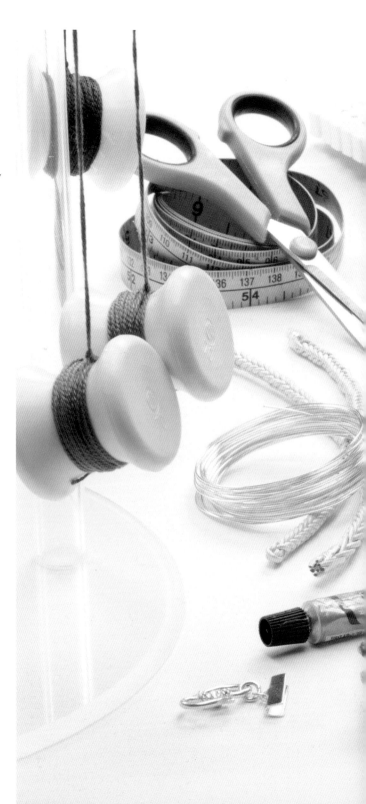

Nylon-jaw pliers (4)

These pliers have a softer material covering the metal jaws to prevent damage to softer wires and findings. They are available as round-nose or flat-nose pliers.

Crimp pliers

Available in a three sizes – micro, regular and macro – these pliers are used to close crimps neatly around bead stringing wire in particular. Match the pliers to the thickness of wire and crimp size.

Split-ring pliers

With a specially-designed tip for opening split-rings, these will definitely help prevent broken nails!

Awl (5)

An awl is useful for pushing and easing cords and braids into metal findings.

Warp posts (6)

Clamp over the edge of the work surface and set a particular distance apart for winding long lengths of cord.

Other essentials

You might find these items in your toolbox already; they will be useful when knotting and braiding.

Scissors

Keep two or three different sizes of scissors specially for cutting threads and cord and don't use them for cutting paper as this will blunt the blades very quickly. Medium scissors are ideal for cutting thread and cords to length and small embroidery scissors with sharp points are perfect for trimming ends neatly.

Needles

There are all sorts of needles that can make it easier to finish braids and knotting or thread beads.

Sewing needles (A) A selection of different sized sewing needles will allow you to sew through braids or secure ends after wrapping. Sharps have a small eye but are quite sturdy and can be used to stitch small seed beads into tougher cords. Embroidery needles have longer eyes to make them easier to thread.

Tapestry needles (B) These have a relatively blunt tip and large eye and are useful for stringing bigger beads onto cord or for manoeuvring knots into position.

Beading needles (C) Fine beading needles are used to add seed beads and other small beads to braids or to cover joins. A size 10 needle is ideal for size 11 seed beads and a size 12 or 13 for size 15 seed beads. Keep a good stock as the finer needles in particular can bend and break.

Twisted wire needles (D) You can make your own needles by looping fine wire over the jaws of round-nose pliers and twisting the tails together. Alternatively, they can be bought in a range of sizes to string beads onto cord or thread or to pull thread or cords through braids to work or neaten ends.

Big eye needles (E) These long needles with two pointed ends are useful for stringing beads onto multi-strands of fine threads, but avoid using to pull cords through a tight space as the two fine rods that make the needle will split apart at the soldered end.

Pins

Dressmaker's pins Useful for marking braids at a particular length, for spacing beads or embellishments, or to position wrapped threads.

Map pins These short pins with ball ends are perfect for securing cords and threads when working macramé. Pin into a cork board or sheet of foam core.

Adhesives

There are a range of different glues that will come in useful for sticking cords and threads, and for making jewellery and other accessories. Choose the correct adhesive to suit the materials you are sticking and remember to leave for 24 hours for the glue to set properly before using.

Jewellery glue

Glues such as G-S Hypo Cement and E6000 are specially made for jewellery. The glue sets but stays pliable so that it is less prone to crack and break off over time. The G-S Hypo Cement has a fine nozzle ideal for applying a tiny amount for a neat finish, otherwise use a cocktail stick to apply the glue.

Superglue

These instant glues can be useful as you don't need to hold the material in position until the glue sets. The gel version is less likely to run and it's easier to be accurate and apply a tiny amount. Take care as these cyanoacrylate glues will bond skin.

Epoxy resin

A two-part adhesive that is very good for sticking cords into metal findings. Wipe surfaces with nail polish remover to remove greasy fingerprints before you apply the adhesive. A 5-minute epoxy resin shortens the drying time and one that dries clear is less likely to be visible when used.

D

E

A

B

C

GENERAL TECHNIQUES

Making the braids or knotting is just the first stage in the process when making a piece of jewellery or an accessory and you then need to finish the piece in an attractive, neat and professional way. These general techniques can be used or adapted for many of the projects in the book. For specific finishing techniques for plaiting and Kumihimo braiding see Finishing Techniques for Braiding.

Adding a jump ring

Jump rings are one of the most useful jewellery findings. Usually round, they can also be oval – a shape with more stability as the elongated ring tends to remain in one position.

1 Hold the jump ring with two pairs of flat-nose pliers either side of the join; tilt one pair towards you and the other away from you. Reverse the process to close the ring again.

2 To tension the jump ring so that the ends butt together, use pliers to push the ends slightly so that they overlap on one side and then the other. Pull back and the ends will spring together.

You can temper (harden) jump rings by opening and closing ring a few times (see step 1). Don't overdo it or the ring will snap.

Making a plain loop

Use a headpin no thinner than 0.6mm (24 swg) wire to make this style of loop so that it is strong enough to keep its round shape when it is in use.

Making a bead link

Make a plain loop on one end of the wire, or start with an eyepin. Add the beads, then follow Making a Plain Loop to make a loop at the other end.

1 Pick up the beads required onto the headpin and trim the tail to about 7–12mm (⅜–½in) – the length depends on the thickness of the wire and the size of the loop required – and bend it over at 90 degrees.

2 Hold the tip of the wire with round-nose pliers and rotate the pliers to bend the wire part-way around the tip of the jaws; the distance from the tip of the pliers determines the size of the loop.

3 Reposition the pliers by flipping your wrist, then continue to rotate the wire around until the tip touches the wire again and the loop is upright and central, like a lollipop.

Making a wrapped loop

You can use a thinner wire for this loop as the wire wrapping makes it more secure. Use longer headpins for this technique – you'll need at least 3cm (1⅛in) of wire above the last bead.

1 String the beads on the headpin and use snipe-nose pliers to bend the wire at a right angle above the last bead leaving a small gap for the wrapping.

2 Hold the wire close to the bead with round-nose pliers, then wrap the tail all the way round to form a loop. Bring the wire right round so that it is at right angles to the wire threaded through the beads.

3 Hold the loop securely in flat-nose pliers and wind the tail around the stem covering the gap between the bead and the loop. You can use another pair of pliers to wind the tail, then trim neatly using flush wire cutters.

Joining a wrapped loop to a solid ring

If you are attaching the wrapped loop to chain, a solid ring or another wrapped loop, use this technique.

1 Form the loop following Making a Wrapped Loop, steps 1 and 2, stopping before you wrap the tail. Feed the tail into the chain link or solid ring so that the loop is sitting where it should be.

2 Use snipe-nose pliers to hold the loop securely, then wind the tail around the gap above the bead using another pair of pliers to give you more purchase if necessary.

3 Trim the tail close to the wrapped wire. Use the very tip of the wire cutters, flat side towards the wrapping, to get the neatest result.

FINISHING TECHNIQUES

Knotting and braiding techniques all have at least one raw end that needs to be neatened or covered in some way to make a piece of jewellery, accessory or other item. Traditional techniques such as whipping or button knots use the knotting or braiding cord itself to cover the raw ends, or you can use a wide range of different findings and fastenings specially designed for the purpose.

Neatening the raw ends

Cords and braids tend to splay out at the end, so it is essential that the end be neatened in some way to enable you to fit it into a finding. There are various techniques that you can use to neaten raw ends and which one you choose will depend on the number of strands and type of material being used.

Melting

When using nylon knotting cord or paracord neaten the end first by holding it for a second or two in a flame – a household gas lighter is sufficient – to melt the end and fuse the raw ends.

Sewing

Braids can be stitched to secure the bundles of cords before the finding is attached. This is particularly suitable for rectangular end caps and ribbon crimps.

Before you trim the braid, sew across near the end using strong beading or sewing thread, working running stitches in one direction, then sewing back across. Sew in the ends with a couple of tiny backstitches.

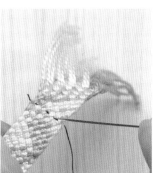

Wrapping

Use strong beading or sewing thread, or fine wire, to finish braids or cord ends prior to attaching a finding. This technique adds very little extra width to the cord.

1 Working near the end of the cord, wrap the thread or wire neatly around near the end of the cord so that the wrapping is even and the starting end is trapped underneath. Don't overwrap or it will be too bulky.

2 Use a sewing needle to stitch the tail under the wrapped threads. Trim the tail, then, if necessary, across the top of the cord too.

Whipping

You can use a thicker cord for a decorative whipped end. This technique can also be used on a single end or over a double rope as shown here to create a loop.

1 Make a loop from thin cord and lay it on top side at the end of the braid or looped braid. Wrap the working end around the braid from the bottom and over both loop cords several times.

2 Continue to wrap the fine cord to create a single depth of wrapping. Keeping the cords neat and tidy as you wrap, insert the working end into the loop.

3 Pull the tail of the thin cord loop gently and then tug to bury the loop under the whipping. Trim both tails neatly.

Finishing with cord ends, end caps and cones

There are many different shapes and styles of cord end, end cap or cone suitable for finishing raw ends and some of the vast array is explored in Essential Equipment. The shape of the finding and the type of cord or braid will determine the techniques used. For specific techniques for macramé and Kumihimo, see Finishing Techniques for Knotting and Finishing Techniques for Braiding.

Cord ends and end caps

Cord ends are small metal findings designed to cover one or several fine raw ends. End caps which can be square, rectangular or round, are larger than cord ends, and suitable for a thick rope or braid. Both sizes either have a solid ring or hole so that a fastening can be attached. It is important to match the internal width or dimensions of the finding to the diameter or size of the cord or braid.

Fitting an end cone or cap

1 Wrap the end of the braid (or bundle of cords) with fine sewing or beading thread (see Wrapping), making sure the wrapping is not too deep so that it will be hidden inside the end cap; trim neatly.

2 Using a cocktail stick, smear a little glue (E6000 or G-S Hypo Cement) around the inside rim of the end cap, also adding a drop or two inside at the bottom. Avoid getting glue on the outside of the finding.

3 Push the braid (or cords) into the end cap, making sure that it is straight and that no raw ends are protruding; you can use a dressmaker's pin to tuck any stray fibres inside. Repeat at the other end, then leave to dry for 24 hours..

Adding a loop to an end cone or cap

Some styles of end cone or cap have a hole at the end rather than a ring. You can attach a piece of wire or a headpin to the braid then make a plain or wrapped loop. Choose the style to suit the technique, so that the raw ends are all covered and the edge of the end cap or cone fits snugly around the braid or cords.

1 Wrap or whip the end of the braid or bundle of cords with thread or fine wire making sure that the end cap will still fit over. Bend the headpin over about 6mm (¼in) from the end and insert it under the wrapping as shown.

2 Bring the end of the headpin out in the centre of the braid end. Use snipe-nose pliers to bend the end of the headpin back up over the wrapping towards the braid end.

3 Add glue inside the end cap or cone and insert the braid feeding the headpin through the hole.

4 Work a plain or wrapped loop on the end of the headpin (see General Techniques). If the hole is large, you can add a small bead to plug the gap before making the loop.

KNOTTING

Even if you are a beginner to the craft of knotting, you probably know more than you realize. Do you remember when you learnt to tie your shoelaces, or when you last fastened a rope around a pole, or simply tied a knot at the end of a sewing thread? The chances are you will have used a reef knot, a half-hitch knot or an overhand knot without even thinking about it, and you probably know a few more besides. In fact all knots are based on two very simple knots – the overhand and the half-hitch – so learn to tie these and any of the techniques featured in this section will be possible, and there are some fabulous projects included to get you started.

This section features three main chapters exploring the decorative possibilities of knot-making, whether you are making individually-worked knots, knotted braids, or exploring macramé, you can work through each chapter building up your skills as you go, or simply dip in and out as you choose.

Each technique is clearly explained with fully illustrated step-by-step instructions, and while the technique samples have been worked with standard cords for maximum clarity, the project ideas show how the beauty of the knots can be enhanced by choosing different cords or threads, thicker or thinner, depending on how you choose to use the design. You'll also discover how the addition of beads can enhance the techniques for even more stunning results.

But before you begin exploring the possibilities, take the time to read Knotting Basics, which outlines the key knotting terms and basic knots you'll need to know to get the most from the knotting techniques.

Knotting Basics

You will find that the instructions for making decorative knots are much easier to follow if you know the terms commonly used. Also, it is a good idea to get to grips with the basic knots used before you make a start on any particular technique.

> Did you know that there are three different types of knotting, although we generally use 'knot' to describe all three? A 'bend' is used to tie two different cords together, a 'hitch' to tie a cord around another object, and a 'knot' to tie one or both ends of a cord around itself, often at its end, to form a stopper.

Knotting terms

Take a moment or two to familiarize yourself with the knotting terms frequently used in step instructions, most of which are illustrated below.

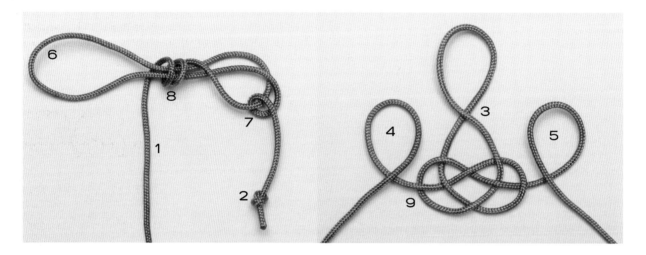

Working end (1) The end of the cord that you are using to tie the knot.

Starting end (2) The opposite end to the working end – if you begin in the middle of a cord both ends are working ends.

Cross point (3) Where one cord crosses over the other. An overhand cross point is when the working end is on top, and when the working end is underneath it is an underhand cross point.

Clockwise loop (4) Sometimes referred to as an overhand loop, this is where the working end goes around clockwise and over itself again.

Anticlockwise (counter-clockwise) loop (5) Sometimes referred to as an underhand loop, this is where the working end goes around anticlockwise and over itself again.

U-shaped bend (6) Also known as a bight, this is often made as a way to weave cord through the knot.

Circled (7) The cord passes around one or more strands in the knot.

Coiled (8) The cord wraps around one or more strands several times.

Weave (9) To go over and under successive cords in a knot with a working end or U-shaped bend.

Firm up Tighten the knot until the cords are secure, but not so tight that the knot is distorted.

Core cord This is a stationary cord inside other threads and cords. In macramé the core cords can become working cords and vice versa; in Kumihimo a hollow braid can be worked around a core cord.

Base cord This cord often forms the basic shape of a necklace or can be substituted for a finding, such as a solid ring, fastening or bar. The working cords are usually attached to the base cord with lark's head knots (see Nesting Lark's Head Knot).

Basic knots

Learn to tie these basic knots off by heart as they are used time and time again for the projects as well as creating more complex knots throughout this chapter.

Reef (square) knot

This is used to join two cord ends of even thickness and it can be loosened if required by

tugging one end back over the knot. It is the basis for the square knot in macramé.

Pass the left cord over the right and tuck under, then pass the right cord over the left and under, to bring the cord up through the loop on the left.

Overhand knot

This simple knot can be tied at the end of a cord as a stopper or for a reminder of the starting end, or it can be used

to tie a bundle of cords together in preparation for plaiting or braiding.

Working over the thumb, make a clockwise loop and bring the working thread up through the loop.

Slip knot

The base of many knotted braids, the slip knot is tied so that the working end is adjustable.

Make an anticlockwise loop and hold the cord at the cross point (at the bottom) in your left hand. Bring the working cord behind the loop and pull a U-shaped bend through. Pull the short starting end to firm up the knot and the working end to adjust the size of loop.

Lark's head

This knot is used to attach one cord to another, or to attach a cord to a bar or to a ring as shown here, and it is the most commonly used knot for starting macramé projects.

Fold one cord in half and pass the loop you have made through the ring from front to back. Pass the tails through the loop and pull up to tighten. To make a reverse lark's head knot, pass the loop through the ring from the reverse side and complete the knot by passing the tails through the loop again.

Half-hitch

One of the basic macramé knots, worked over another cord as shown here, or over

a ring or bar. It is often used in pairs to secure finer cords or threads.

Take one cord and pass the working end under the other cord and behind the starting end to make one half-hitch. Make a second loop in the same way passing the working end through the loop between the two half-hitches for extra security.

Carrick bend

This knot can be worked with two cords as described, or using just one thread, and it is the base of many decorative knots.

Make a clockwise loop in one cord with the tails on the left. Lay the second cord behind the loop with the starting end at the bottom right. Pass the working end over then under the tails of the first cord and then weave it over and under cords to come out at the top of the right loop again.

INDIVIDUAL KNOTS

Individual knots are slightly more advanced, using some of the elements of the basic knots to create different decorative knots. Sometimes these individual knots are tied singly but they can often be tied one after the other to create a braid. Try tying the knots with a variety of materials or add beads for different effects.

Basic Knots

The simplest of knots can make the most attractive jewellery. Overhand knots can be tied to separate or attach beads and reef knots make a quick and easy bracelet, and there are many more ideas in this section for getting the most from basic knots.

Reef knot

When working a reef knot, cord too thick for tying intricate knots can be transformed into a simple and effective design, ideal for making a pretty bracelet.

1 Cut two 25cm (10in) lengths of 6mm cord and tie a reef knot (see Knotting Basics). Adjust the knot so that all the ends are the same length, then pull gently to firm up.

2 Check the length of the bracelet allowing for the fastening, trim the cord ends, then attach both cords at each end into the fastening using strong jewellery glue.

Carrick bend

This sailor's knot is traditionally used to tie thick ropes together, but when tied with strands of double cord and allowed to lie flat it makes a pretty decorative knot.

1 Cut two lengths of 6mm paracord measuring 60cm (24in) in two different colours; fold each in half. Take one of the double cords (pink) and make a clockwise loop. Lay the second double cord (grey) behind the first (pink) loop and bring the working (folded) end over and under the tails of the first (pink) cord as shown.

2 Weave back over the first (pink) loop passing the second (grey) cord under itself before it comes back up and over the end of the first (pink) loop. Adjust the knot so that all the ends are about the same length and the knot is firm.

3 Check the length of the bracelet allowing for the fastening and trim the cords. Apply jewellery glue between the cords at both ends and leave to dry. Attach a ribbon crimp end and a jewellery fastening at each end (see Finishing Techniques).

> If your cord is silky or slippery the knot may not stay firm – use a little glue or a few tiny stitches sewn on the reverse side to secure it.

Overhand knots

The overhand knot looks fabulous tied into a rustic leather cord; it can be used to separate beads and attach charms, and even for a simple sliding fastening.

★ Use overhand knots to anchor a bead on a length of cord or to space beads along the length of the leather. Choose cord to suit the size of the bead hole.

★ When designing with two or more strands of cord, one of the strands could be thinner to pass through small-hole beads before tying all the strands together with an overhand knot.

★ Use an overhand knot to attach a jump ring charm or chain along the length of the cord. Tie the knot through links on the same side of the chain to prevent it twisting.

★ Loop two lengths of cord in opposite directions through a washer-style bead or button, then tie with an overhand knot at each side to secure.

★ Create a simple beaded tassel by tying a bundle of cords together with an overhand knot; add a bead on each strand and tie an overhand knot above and below the knot to secure it.

★ For a sliding fastening lay two cord ends in opposite directions and, at each end, tie an overhand knot over the other cord and firm up each. Pull the tails to open and the main cord to close.

Thicker cords, such as paracord and eco nappa leather, look fabulous when tied in basic knots like the reef knot and Carrick bend to create simple bracelets. The same designs would also look great tied in your own Kumihimo braid (see Kumihimo): any of the round or hollow braids would be suitable so long as you choose braiding threads carefully to achieve the correct thickness for the finished braid.

Lark's head knot

Often overlooked, this is one of the most useful knots for making jewellery and accessories – single or multiple lark's head knots can be used to make attractive jewellery designs.

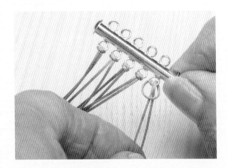

★ Tie lark's head knots through the rings in a slide fastening ready to work a wide panel of macramé to make a cuff bracelet.

★ Use the lark's head knot to attach a cord to a solid ring to make a pendant that can be further embellished with jump rings and bead charms.

★ Secure a ring, or other shape, with a lark's head knot on either side, then secure the ends in a fastening for a simple bracelet.

Nesting lark's head knot

The nesting lark's head knot is useful if using two colours of cord when knotting or working macramé.

★ Tie a lark's head knot with the first cord (light pink), then lay the second cord (dark pink) horizontally below the first knot, taking the ends around the back of the base cord and tuck into the loop created.

When the multiple lark's head knot bracelet is the length you require, you can use the thinner cords to attach a fastening, such as a button, or alternatively, glue the cord ends into a toggle fastening as shown here. Feed the U-bend into the metal slider. Check the loop is large enough for the toggle and glue in place.

Multiple lark's head knots

Working the knots one after the other uses a slightly different technique, as you have to weave one tail around the core cord so that it follows the correct path to make a lark's head knot.

> These techniques work well with a 1mm cord tied to a 3–4mm core cord, as used for the samples shown.

Single core technique

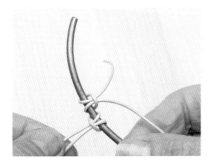

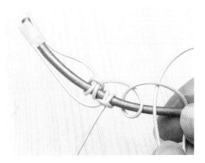

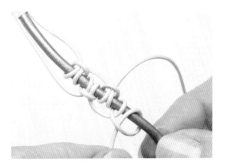

1 Use a lark's head knot to attach a thin cord to one end of a thicker core cord; tie on a second length of thin cord with a lark's head knot facing in the other direction.

2 With the first working end, work a half-hitch (see Basic Knots) over the core cord. Pass the working end under the core cord again and back up through the loop to complete a third lark's head knot.

3 Continue working from side to side working one lark's head knot at a time with alternate cords. You can add beads on the large loops down each side.

Double core technique

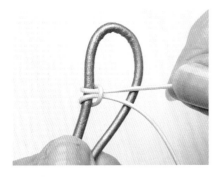

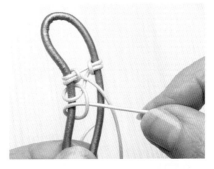

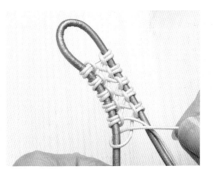

1 For a bracelet length: tie a lark's head knot near the middle of a 40cm (16in) length of thick leather cord. Bend this core cord in half and take the top working cord of the lark's head knot across and over the other half of the core cord.

2 Make a second lark's head knot on the right-hand side of the loop as Single Core Technique, step 2, then pass the right-hand working cord diagonally across and over the left-hand core cord. Tie a lark's head knot. Take the left-hand working cord across and over the right-hand core cord. Tie another lark's head knot.

3 Continue with the criss-cross pattern of lark's head knots all the way down the core cords. You can adjust the size of the top loop to accommodate a button or toggle.

> Decide whether to keep the same diagonal cord on top between the knots or to alternate them to create a slightly different centre pattern.

Chinese Knots

Many different cultures tie knots but it is the Chinese who are the best known for their decorative knots. The knots featured in this section are fairly simple but many of these can be combined to create more complex structures. Chinese knots were often tied as good luck charms or to ward off evil spirits.

Button knot

Button knots are very decorative and can be used in place of a round bead, or as an end stopper. Tying with one end of a single cord is shown, but two cords or a doubled cord can also be used.

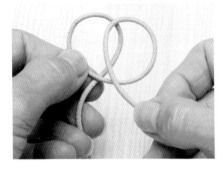

1 Make an anticlockwise loop with the working end on the right. Make a second anticlockwise loop over the first, then hold firmly at the cross point at the bottom of the loops.

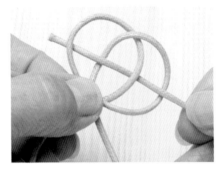

2 Weave the working end (right-hand tail) through the two loops from right to left, going over, under, over, under, to come out the other side.

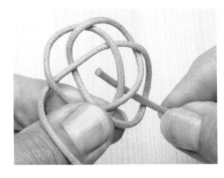

3 Bring the working end back round over the starting end, pass down through the loop and under the cross point, then bring the working end up in the middle of the knot.

4 At this point hold the bottom loops between finger and thumb and turn the sides down to create a ring shape or toggle around the tip of your finger. Pull the tails to firm up slightly.

5 Pull the tails to tighten the knot until a loop of cord pops up from the side of the toggle. Work around the knot, pushing one end of the loop down and pull through.

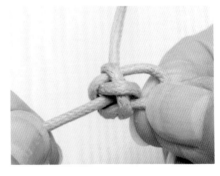

6 Keep pushing the knot back down, working around the button knot in the same direction until it reaches one of the ends. Take your finger out and repeat the loop pulling process until the knot is firm.

> Working around your finger prevents the knot from collapsing and becoming tangled, especially when working with a soft cord like rattail.

Moving a button knot

When working button knots side by side or next to a bead, it can be difficult to position them exactly, so this technique enables you to move one knot to another.

1 Tie the first button knot in the correct position, then tie a second button knot so that it ends up fairly close to the first, but don't pull it too tight.

2 Turn the knot around until you find the loop that emerges as the core thread on the left-hand side, and pull the loop through until the second button knot is moved across to butt up against the first.

3 Work around the knot pulling adjacent loops through until you reach the working cord at the other end, repeating if necessary to firm up the knot to make it the same size as the first knot. Tie more button knots, moving them along the cord.

Sliding button knot fastening

Use button knots for a decorative sliding fastening for a necklace or bracelet. Two colours of cord are shown for clarity but for a necklace or bracelet the cords will be the same colour.

2 Arrange the first button knot on the left-hand side with a long end of the other cord out to the right. Begin by forming the first two anticlockwise loops around the other cord (shown here in a contrast colour).

1 Near the end of the cord, tie a button knot to the toggle stage (see Button Knot, step 4). Pass the other end of the cord (shown here in a contrast colour) through the middle of the toggle in the opposite direction to the short tail, then continue to pull loops through the button knot (see Button Knot, steps 5 and 6) to make a small firm knot.

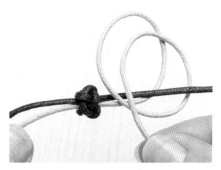

3 Continue to finish the button knot and then work the loops through to firm up the second button knot around the other cord. Pull the knots to close the fastening and the main cords to open it.

4 Apply a little glue inside the second button knot where the tail emerges and trim when dry, then secure the first knot in the same way. Do make sure the button knots will slide as the glue dries.

Double coin knot

The double coin knot is a variation of the Carrick bend (see Knotting Basics), and its shape mimics a classic Chinese design motif of two overlapping antique coins.

1 Make a clockwise loop at least 20cm (8in) from the starting end of the cord so that the cross point is on the left.

2 Holding the cross point in your left hand, bring the working end around so that it forms a U-shaped bend to finish running down across the loop.

3 Change to hold the loops and working end cord in your right hand. Pass the working end under the starting end as shown.

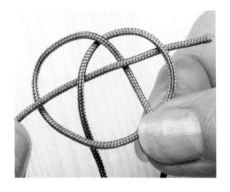

4 Weave the tail of the working end over, under, over and under the cords to emerge out of the right loop.

5 Pull the working end through till all three loops are the same size, before you begin to shape the knot.

6 Adjust by pulling the ends and working the cord through to create a fairly loose knot that is firm enough to be stable.

If you are using a soft cord or slightly frayed end, create a U-shaped bend with the working end before weaving it through the loops in step 4.

Double coin knots can be tied with other knots such as the prosperity knot to create interesting braids.

Double coin knot with Carrick bends

Begin with a double coin knot, then work a series of Carrick bends (see Knotting Basics) to create a wide knotted band, adjusting the spacing in between as you wish.

1 Begin in the centre of a long cord and tie a double coin knot (see Double Coin Knot). Make an anticlockwise loop with the right cord, lay the left cord down across the loop and hold where the cords cross.

2 To complete the first Carrick bend, bring the left cord under the right cord and then down through the space under the double coin knot. Weave under, over and under across the loops.

3 Firm up, adjusting the length of the 'legs' between the knots. Begin to tie the next Carrick bend with a clockwise loop on the left cord and lay the right cord over the top. Alternate the start direction of each knot until you have the required length.

> If you work the knots beginning with a clockwise loop on the left cord each time the series of knots will not lie as flat.

When working the double coin knot with Carrick bends you can adjust the spacing between the knots to create large gaps in between, ideal for a belt, or butt them close together for a cuff-style bracelet. For step-by-step instructions for making the Double Coin Knot Cuff, see Projects.

Toggle

The toggle is a version of a Turk's head knot worked from a double coin knot base, and its size can be varied according to the thickness of cord and number of times the cord is woven through.

1 Tie a double coin knot (see Double Coin Knot) so that the left-hand starting end is short and the right-hand working end longer. Bring the working end around and pass it down through the first loop where the starting end emerges.

2 Following the same path as the starting end, weave the working end under, over and under again to emerge at the other side of the loops, and pull it out over the edge of the right-hand loop.

3 Bring the working cord around and continue to follow the path of the starting end as in step 2, keeping the cord to the inside as you go around. Continue until you have doubled up all the cords.

For a beaded napkin ring, transfer strings of size 6 seed beads onto a 1.5m (1²/₃yd) length of 1mm aluminium wire. Make a loop in the wire at each end to secure the beads, then tie the toggle (see Toggle). Carry on weaving the working end through the toggle to make three rows of beaded wire. Remove any excess beads and twist the two wire ends together, trimming neatly on the inside.

4 At this point insert your finger in the middle of the knot and hold between finger and thumb, so that it forms a ring rather than a flat knot. Pull the loop between the two ends to begin to tighten the toggle.

5 Work around the toggle pulling the cord through one loop at a time until the toggle is the size required. Tuck the ends into the centre of the toggle, trim and glue on the inside.

Button ball

Also known as a monkey's fist, this round ball-shaped knot is often worked flat, but using the toggle as a base makes it easier to firm up the knot for a good round shape.

1 Follow Toggle, steps 1–4 to create a double-row toggle. Pass the starting end under two cords as shown to emerge in the middle of the ring. Tie an overhand knot on the end and trim the tail.

2 Pull cords through until the overhand knot is flush on the inside. Pull the loop next to the working end and work around pulling up the slack as you go.

3 Tuck the working end under two loops to emerge in the middle of the toggle-shaped knot. Continue pulling the loops gently – as the toggle tightens it will form into a ball shape around the overhand knot – until the knot is firm.

Take your time pulling the loops and taking up the slack to get the roundest ball shape.

Worked as a three-row toggle, button ball knots make great gift box 'handles'. Make or buy little gift boxes and cover with pretty paper. Pierce a hole in the lid or drawer and thread the tail of the button ball through. Tie an overhand knot on the inside to secure.

Prosperity knot

As this knot resembles several double coin knots worked together, it is said to bring wealth and prosperity to anyone who ties or incorporates it onto their garments.

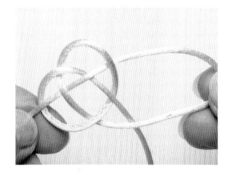

1 Begin by tying a double coin knot in the centre of a length of cord (see Double Coin Knot). Pull the side loops out one at a time to about 3cm (1¼in) on each side (this will vary depending on the thickness of your cord).

2 Bring the loops down below the working ends at either side and adjust the weaving at the top of the knot so that it is firm.

3 Holding the working ends out of the way twist the left side over the right on each of the long loops.

4 Tuck the loop on the left up through the back of the loop on the right. Bring the right working end down and under the top loop so that it is lying between the two twisted loops.

5 Tuck the top twisted loop down through the bottom twisted loop to trap the working end. Re-adjust the knot cords to make the knot more even.

6 Bring the left working end down and up through the remaining loop in the middle of the left side. Weave over, under, over and under to come out at the right-hand side. Adjust the knot until it is firm.

The finished prosperity knot looks beautiful on its own worked in a soft silky rattail as shown, with just a pendant bead attached, or several can be tied one after the other to make a strap or band.

The prosperity knot has a slightly pointed end a little like the end of a belt, so this was the inspiration for working a firm rectangular belt panel from leather cord, adaptable to the size of your waist. For step-by-step instructions for making the Prosperity Knot Belt, see Projects.

Flat button knot

Depending on the cord used to tie the flat button knot, it can be used as a pretty button, brooch, earring or cuff links.

1 Make a clockwise loop in a P-shape and bring the working end down through the loop to make another loop the same size as the first. Hold in your left hand on the left cross point.

2 Loop the working end (right-hand cord) around to the right and weave it under, over, under and over through the loops to come out at the left-hand side.

3 Bring the working end around again over the starting end and weave across the right of the knot, going under, over and then under the last two cords.

4 Firm up by pulling on the two ends, then each of the loops in turn, pulling up the slack as you work through the knot.

5 The finished flat button knot.

Two-tone flat button knot

To make a two-tone knot, tie a flat button knot with two cords at once, or feed a second cord through a single knot before you start to firm it up.

Soft cords like rattail make a flatter knot than firmer round cords.

Pipa knot

This traditional Chinese knot was used to make decorative toggle fastenings for Oriental clothing, with a pipa knot loop one side and a button knot on the other.

1 Make a clockwise loop so that the working end is on the left. Make another loop beneath to create a figure of eight with the working end on top as shown. (The bottom loop should be the finished size at this stage.)

3 Loop the working end back around to the top so that the cord is sitting inside the bottom loop. Repeat step 2 taking the cord behind the small loop and inside the large loop again.

2 Holding the bottom loop so that it stays the same size, loop the working end around the small loop at the top and then back across itself again.

4 Continue to wrap the working end in a figure of eight until only a small hole is left in the middle of the bottom loops. Pass the working end down through the hole and firm up.

> Based on a figure of eight, the simple structure of the pipa knot makes it ideal for working in wire.

Open-loop pipa knot

You can make the bottom loops much larger so that you finish with a tightly packed top section and a larger hole in the middle. To finish this style of knot, take the working end down through the hole in the middle; turn the knot over and feed the tail up through the small loops at the back of the knot. You can pull the top loop through too, to make a pendant.

The longer loops of the open-loop pipa knot are perfect for attaching beads. Embellish the earrings with tiny pearls attached with headpins to the bottom loop. The pipa knot can be worked in cord or leather thong or a soft aluminium wire as shown here.

Flower Knots

Flower knots can be tied with a varying number of loops from two up to eight or more. The actual moves are the same but the repetition isn't clear until you are making more than four petals and so there are step-by-step instructions for two, three and four petal knots as well as the flower brocade knot.

Two-petal flower knot

With two loops (or petals), the knot looks like a bow. It is easier to tie with a matt cord, which is less slippery than the satin cord shown here.

1 In your left-hand, make a U-shaped bend with the working end at the bottom. Make a second U-shaped bend and pass it through the first. Hold the first U-shaped bend taut to create the first petal.

2 Change hands so that you are holding the cross point with the right hand. Pass the working end down through the loop formed by the second U-shaped bend.

3 Pass the cord over the starting end and down through the bottom loop.

4 Take the cord under and back up through the second U-shaped bend again.

5 Pull the tails gently to firm up and adjust until the two loops are the right size for the bow.

Tie a two-petal flower knot using a rustic leather cord and attach a chain with jump rings (see General Techniques) to make a delicate, pretty necklace.

Three-petal flower knot

If tied in the middle of a long cord, the three petals make an attractive trefoil shape. Hung upside down it makes a simple and attractive pendant necklace.

1 Work the first petal following Two-petal Flower Knot, step 1, then make another U-shaped bend with the working end and pass it through the first U-shaped bend. Pull the petal just formed to firm up the knot so far.

2 Change hands to hold the cross point in your right hand. Pass the working end down through the third U-shaped bend (petal), over the starting end and down through the bottom right loop.

3 Pass the working end behind the petals and back up through the third U-shaped bend (petal) on the left again. Pull the loop just formed to firm the knot before letting go. Firm up the knot.

4 The finished three-petal flower knot; it can be used as a pretty stopper for beads, or turn it upside down and hang bead charms from one or more of the loops for a pendant.

By pulling in the previous U-shaped bend each time, you have more control over the loop size.

Cross knot

The cross knot is similar to the three-petal flower knot but without the petals. It's a very stable knot that can be used as a decorative link to tie two strands together.

1 Take two cords and make a cross shape. Make a U-shaped bend with the horizontal cord on the left side and tuck under the vertical cord to create an S-shape.

2 Hold in your left hand, and pass the bottom working end of the vertical cord behind the horizontal cords, passing it down through the U-shaped bend at bottom right and out over itself again.

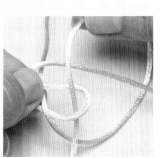

3 Pull all four cord ends gently to remove the slack and then work the loops through if necessary to firm up the knot.

Work the knot with two cords as shown, or fold a cord in half and work the knot with both ends.

Cross knot with beads

Beads can be added on one or both of the strands between the knots to make a bracelet or necklace. String beads onto one or both tails below the cross knot. Tie the next knot underneath adjusting the spacing as required before firming up the knot.

Four-leaf clover

The four-leaf clover is essentially a four-petal flower knot. The secret to the success for making this knot in your hand is to ensure each U-shaped bend is pulled taut to hold the next one securely.

1 Make a U-shaped bend with the working end on the right. Make a second U-shaped bend with the working end and pass it through the first. Adjust the first U-shaped bend to hold the second one taut.

2 Repeat the process: make a U-shaped bend with the working end and pass through the previous U-shaped bend. Pull the left side of the loop just formed to firm up the knot so far and create the second leaf.

3 Adjust the knot in your hand so that you are holding the firmed up centre at the last-made loop. Repeat step 2, pulling the left side of the loop just formed to firm up the knot.

4 Change hands. Pass the working end down through the last U-shaped bend, over the starting end and down through the next leaf. Bring the working end under the starting end and back up through the leaf on the left.

5 The last loop formed is not a leaf but a U-shaped bend that gets pulled taut. Pull the working end and the last loop to firm up the knot, then adjust the other loops for leaves of the same size.

The ring formation of the flower brocade knot, worked in Russian braid, makes an attractive bezel for a cabochon stone. To make a brooch, stick the cabochon stone onto a circle of stiff interfacing, stitch the knot in place and back with faux suede; sew a brooch pin above the centre line.

Flower brocade knot

The flower brocade knot is tied in exactly the same way as the other flower knots, but once more than five or six petals are tied it transforms into a ring.

1 Make a U-shaped bend and pass a second U-shaped bend through the first. Pull the starting end to firm up the knot, then stick a narrow piece of tape around the starting end and the left side of the first loop as shown.

Adding the piece of tape stabilizes the start of the knot and enables you to work the rest of the knot in your hand while keeping the tension and size of the petals even.

2 Adjust the loop under the cross point to the size of petal required. *Make a U-shaped bend with the working end and pass through the U-shaped bend at the top.

3 Pull the left side of the loop you've just formed to firm up the knot so far, then pull the left side of the U-shaped bend to re-size the petal.

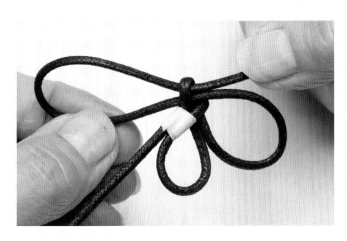

4 Pull the working end to reduce the last U-shaped bend and repeat from *. As you add more petals hold the knot at the final U-shaped bend so the previous petals are held securely.

5 Repeat from *, adjusting the size of the new petal each time until you have formed a ring, then pass the working end through the last U-shaped bend.

6 Carefully remove the tape from the start end. Pass the working end under the two cords to come out of the first-worked loop, taking it back through the last U-shaped bend. Pull both ends to firm up the knot and form the ring.

Ring Knots

The brocade knot and the Ashoka chakra knot are attractive ring-shaped knots based on the slip knot, which can be used as a pendant or focal point for a bracelet. Depending on the type and thickness of cord used to tie the knots with, you could embellish the rings by adding a bead on the working end before forming each U-shaped bend.

Brocade knot

The brocade knot is a version of the flower brocade knot worked without loops, and is tied in a much simpler way using a slip knot technique.

1 Starting with a slip knot, make a length of chain following the steps for caterpillar knot (see Slip Knot Braids: Caterpillar Knot) but pull the U-shaped bend through each time so that there is no loop. Continue until the cord is the required length to make a ring.

3 Take the working end under the starting end and back up through the end loop on the right. Pull up both ends to firm up the knot and form the ring shape.

2 Pass the working end through the end loop, shown here on the right. Remove the starting end from the start loop. Pass the working end over the starting end and down through the start loop.

> The brocade knot builds on the technique used for the caterpillar knot, so practise that first (Slip Knot Braids: Caterpillar Knot).

You can make the Ashoka chakra knot as a beaded pendant. Once you have made the long loop slip knot and are ready to begin, string metal beads onto the working end. Drop one bead down to the work before you make the next slip knot and continue adding beads before every slip knot thereafter.

Ashoka chakra knot

The Ashoka chakra knot is so called as it has been created to resemble the dharma chakra or wheel of life. The knot is formed over an elongated slip knot, which forms the core.

1 Take a 76cm (30in) length of cord and, leaving a 40cm (16in) working end on the right, make a clockwise loop. Form a U-shaped bend with the starting end and pass it through the loop to make a slip knot.

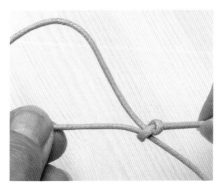

2 Firm up the slip knot and turn it over so that the adjustable starting end is on the left. Pull the slip knot loop through leaving about a 5cm (2in) tail. The length of the long loop can be adjusted later.

3 Make an anticlockwise loop on the right cord end, then make a U-shaped bend with the same end and pass it through the loop to make another slip knot.

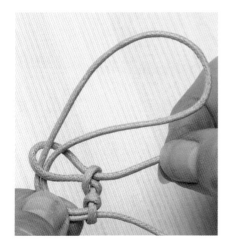

4 Adjust so that the new slip knot is positioned next to the previous slip knot, then insert the long loop into the smaller slip-knot loop and pull the cords taut.

5 Repeat from step 3 until the 'wheel' is the size required. Make sure you adjust the position of each slip knot to butt up against the last. Push the knots down the long loop as you work to create the curved shape.

6 Pass the working end through the end loop. Pass the starting end through the end loop in the opposite direction. Pull the starting end firmly until the slack from the loop is taken up.

> The tighter the knots are butted together, the sharper the curve will be.

KNOTTED BRAIDS

Knotted braids are just a series of individual knots worked one after the other, so although they may look intricate, most are quite easy to make. Although there are only a few basic knots, there are hundreds of knotted braids worked using a variety of techniques: the braids are grouped together so that you can learn one technique, then try the variations.

Basic Knotted Braids

I like to work knots in the hand, but you may find that sometimes it is easier to lay the knotted braids on your work surface or to pin them to foam card. Start with a 2m (2yd) length of cord for any technique.

Snake weave

Sometimes knots are not so much tied as woven or plaited, and the snake weave is a good example of this. Starting with a box knot, it becomes a woven braid resembling Celtic designs based on intertwining snakes.

1 Begin with a box knot: make a loop in the middle of the cord so that the right-hand cord is on the top. Bring the right-hand cord up behind the loop.

2 Weave the left-hand cord over, under and over the looped cord to come out at the right-hand side. Rotate so that the cord tails are facing down.

3 Holding the knot at the cross point at the top, pull the bottom loop down to the required length of the snake weave panel. Pull the cord ends out to the side to firm up the knot at the top.

4 *Twist the bottom loop so that the left side is over the right. Take the right-hand cord over the front of the loop.

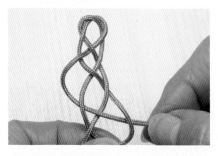

5 Weave the left cord under, over and under the long loop to come out at the right-hand side.

6 Repeat from * until you are close to the bottom of the loop. Adjust the knot to firm up the weave then twist the loop one last time.

7 As shown in step 6, bring the left-hand cord across under the loop again and weave the right-hand cord over, under and over to make a firm woven panel.

★ If the tails are long enough you can weave back down through the braid so that the cords are all doubled up. When weaving back through, you can use a different coloured cord for a two-tone effect.

Celtic bar

This variation of snake weave is more like four-strand plaiting than knotting, and it creates a most attractive braid pattern that can be embellished with beads.

1 Fold the cord ends over in opposite directions with the right-hand cord crossed over the left to form a long loop with the two tails out at either side at least 5cm (2in) longer than the loop. Bring the ends of the loop down to make an inverted V-shape.

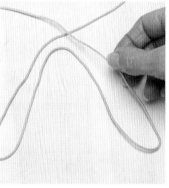

2 Bring the top right cord end down over the right-hand long loop and lay out parallel to the left loop. Bring the top left cord behind the left-hand long loop and then cross the left cord over the right as shown.

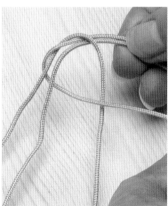

3 *Bring the long loops down, right-hand in front and left-hand behind the single cords and cross the left-hand long loop over the right.

4 Repeat with the single cord, right-hand on top of doubled cords and left-hand behind, then cross the left-hand single cord over the right-hand single cord. Repeat from * until there are only short loops at the bottom.

5 Cross the loops left over right then tuck the right-hand cord into the front of the right loop and the left-hand cord into the back of the left loop to finish.

For an attractive beaded braid, replace the two single cords with a fine Superlon™ or Chinese knotting cord and then string size 8 seed beads on each end. Weave the cords together as a Celtic bar braid, positioning a bead in the centre as the left-hand single cord crosses over the right.

Snake knot

This technique creates an attractive snake-like rope, which if worked in a soft satin cord will be quite pliable, but if worked in a stiffer cord, such as an elastic, will have a much sturdier finish.

1 To make a 15cm (6in) length, cut one piece of cord 20cm (8in) long and two pieces of cord 1m (1⅛yd) long. Tape or tie the cords together so that the shorter piece is in the middle.

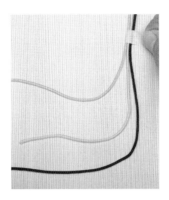

> The snake knot braid can be worked with or without a centre core cord.

2 Make a clockwise loop with the right-hand cord, looping it under the other two cords and back across itself again.

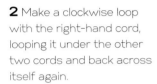

3 Make an anticlockwise loop with the left-hand cord so that it passes under the centre core to come out through the clockwise loop again.

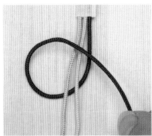

4 Pull the cords up carefully to form a loose knot. Do not pull too tight as you need to get the cord through the loop in the next step.

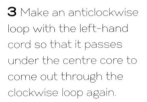

5 Take the right-hand cord under the other two cords and loop it around. Tuck it into the right-hand loop of the knot under the cord that is already there and pull it through.

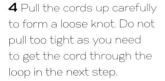

6 Turn the cords over. Loop the right-hand cord around and under the other two cords and down through the bottom of two loops on the right-hand side. Pull the cords through to make a loose knot.

7 Turn the cords over and repeat step 5 with the next right-hand cord as shown in the photograph. Turn over and repeat again, looping the new right-hand cord around and down through the bottom loop on the right.

> When working with a single colour of cord mark one side with a little piece of tape to remind you when to turn over.

8 Continue turning and looping the right-hand cord around and down through the new bottom right-hand loop until the bracelet is the length required.

Work several snake knot ropes using a range of colours and textures of cord. Sew beads across the main rope (see Beaded Knotted Braids) and onto some of the others for an attractive sparkly look. For step-by-step instructions for making the Snake Knot Tie Backs, see Projects.

Switchback Braids

Switchback is one of the easiest of the knotting techniques producing braids with attractive interlocking ridges. The name refers to the way the cord switches direction from side to side. It can be worked with one piece of cord, two colours or two different cords to create a range of effects and textures.

Single cord switchback braid

This technique has an ingenious start sequence and a braid is made with a single cord at each end – perfect for finishing as a simple bracelet.

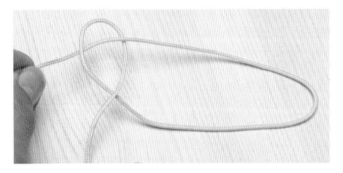

4 Repeat from * stacking the switchback loops firmly against one another. Make sure that the switchback loops on each side are the same size for an even braid.

1 Make a small clockwise loop in the cord about 25cm (10in) from the starting end. Pass the starting end through the small loop so that the length of the large loop is the length of the braiding, approximately 15cm (6in). This can be adjusted later.

2 Turn the work so that the starting end is at the top. *Bring the working end around and under the left loop cord, then over the right loop cord.

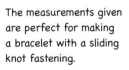
The measurements given are perfect for making a bracelet with a sliding knot fastening.

3 Switch back to bring the working end around the loop on the right side and over the loop on the left side. Hold both loop cords and pull the working end to firm up the knot.

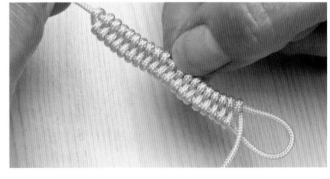

5 Continue until either you reach the end of the loop or the braided section is the length required. Pull on the starting end to take up any slack on the loop and to firm up the braid.

To make a simple bracelet, work about 10cm (4in) of braiding, then make a sliding knot fastening with the 15cm (6in) tails (see Finishing Techniques for Knotting).

Two colour switchback braid

A clever start sequence leaves a pair of cords at each end to make a simple bracelet. Take care as you weave the first few cords as it is not as easy as it seems.

1 Set up the two cords with a clockwise loop as for the single cord switchback braid. * Weave the first colour of cord to the left and then switch back to the right and bring out under the right side of the loop.

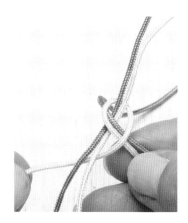

2 Weave the second colour to the left and then switch back to the right in the same way. Pull both cord ends to firm up the knot. Repeat from * until the braid is the length required.

3 To finish the braid, thread both ends between the two loops and then pull on both pairs of cords to firm up the braid.

Two cord switchback braid

Although this looks like the standard switchback braid it is worked with two ends rather than one. Choose a soft 1–2mm cord to wrap around the firmer 3–4mm cord.

1 Fold the thick core cord in half to form an upside down U-shaped bend, and lay it in the middle of a longer thin cord. *Take the left-hand thin cord and pass it over the left-hand thick cord and under the right.

2 Take the right-hand thin cord and pass it over the right-hand thick cord and under the left. Pull the cord ends to firm up the knot.

3 Repeat from * pushing the knots up against one another to create the switchback braid. You can slide the knots up to reduce the size of the loop before continuing.

4 To finish, tie a button on with the thin cord to fasten, or glue all the ends into a metal end cap or fastening.

Stitched switchback strap

This variation looks like the standard switchback braid on the reverse but has an interesting stitch effect running down its length on the front side, which shows up particularly well worked in flat faux suede.

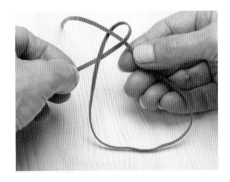

1 Make a large anticlockwise loop with the cord so that the starting end (shown here at the top) is 15cm (6in) and the loop itself is the length required for the finished braid. Bring the working end up through the large loop.

2 Take the working end back across the large loop and then bring it out through the small loop at the top. Pull through to firm up.

3 Bring the working end down and through between the two cords of the large loop. Keep the suede flat and untwisted, then take it out to the right-hand side.

> Check that the shorter starting end is the one that alters the size of the loop so that you can firm up the braid when it is complete.

4 Take the working cord back across the front of the large loop, under the left-hand cord of the large loop, and bring it out above itself. Pull to firm up the knot.

5 Repeat steps 3 and 4, making sure that the suede lies flat as it goes around the large loop and on the vertical stitch.

6 Continue until the braid is the length required, finishing on step 4, then pull on the starting end to firm up. This braid has a single cord at each end, so it can be fastened with an easy sliding knot fastening (see Finishing Techniques for Knotting).

The stitching on this technique can create gaps on the main loop that make it ideal for adding beads (see Beaded Knotted Braids).

The switchback technique and variations work well alongside other knotting techniques such as macramé to make a long wrap bracelet that is secured with a button into the loop at the end. For step-by-step instructions for making the Beaded Switchback Bracelet, see Projects.

Slip Knot Braids

The knots and braids on the following pages are all based on the slip knot (see Basic Knots), a knot that is used when starting a piece of knitting or crochet, so you may already know it. The first knot is usually tied with a short fixed starting end and longer adjustable working end, but this is not always the case and sometimes both ends are the same length, so do read the instructions carefully.

Caterpillar knot

Although one of the simplest knotted braids, often made as children's finger knitting, the caterpillar, or chain knot, looks quite elegant worked in a beautiful silk or rouleau cord.

1 Make an anticlockwise loop so that the starting end is over the working cord. Form a U-shaped bend with the working cord and tuck it into the loop to make a slip knot.

2 Make a U-shaped bend with the working cord and tuck it into the loop as shown. Pull the left side of the top loop to firm up the knot and then adjust the size by pulling the working end.

3 Repeat step 2, adjusting the size of the previous loop each time, until the braid is the length required.

Round brocade knot

Worked in a circle the caterpillar knot becomes the round brocade knot – the resulting ring can be used as a component in jewellery or as a pendant.

Refer to Caterpillar Knot for the technique, but take time to pull the previous loop tight around the U-shaped bend, and then adjust the U-shaped bend to firm up the knot. This process changes the configuration of the knot so that it curves around. Pass the tails through the last loop in opposite directions to form the ring (see Ring Knots).

Use thick shoelaces to make a caterpillar knot braid, adding steel washers from the hardware store to embellish.

Zipper knot

The zipper knot technique is similar to the caterpillar knot, but slip knots alternate from left and right to make a wider, flat braid. The reverse side is different, slightly domed and has a more distinct criss cross pattern.

1 Make a clockwise loop in the middle of the cord. Form a U-shaped bend with the right-hand cord and tuck it into the loop to make a slip knot.

2 Form a U-shaped bend with the left-hand cord and tuck it into the loop. Pull on the right-hand end to firm up the knot.

3 Form a U-shaped bend with the right-hand cord and tuck it into the loop. Pull on the left-hand end to firm up the knot.

4 Repeat steps 2 and 3 until the braid is the length required. Pass both ends through the last loop to finish.

Two-colour zipper knot

This variation can be worked in two contrasting colours as shown in the example below, or in two different shades of the same colour for a more subtle shaded effect.

1 Make a slip knot (see Zipper Knot, step 1) near the end of the first cord, then tuck the starting end of the second cord down through the small loop and tighten the slip knot.

2 Follow and repeat Zipper Knot, steps 2 and 3, swapping from side to side to use each colour alternately to make a two-tone braid. Finish as Zipper Knot, step 4.

Eternal knot

Also known as the mystic or endless knot, the eternal knot is a Celtic knot that can symbolize never-ending love, faith, loyalty or friendship.

1 To make the starting slip knot, make a clockwise loop with the starting end on the left. Make a U-shaped bend with the right-hand working cord and insert into the loop. Pull the starting end to tighten.

2 Tuck the working end into the loop of the slip knot and partially pull through to leave a large loop. Pull the left side of the large loop to tighten the slip knot.

3 Twist the working end side of the large loop forwards to create a figure of eight.

4 Feed the working end from back to front into the end loop of the figure of eight. Carefully firm up the knot.

5 The finished eternal knot:. it looks very attractive worked as a series of knots on a single cord to create a bracelet or necklace.

Tied with a thicker cord, the eternal knot makes a fabulous focal point for a simple bracelet, or it can be finished with end caps or large hole beads to make a pair of pretty earrings.

Spinal knot

The spinal knot has a look of the eternal and caterpillar knots combined, to create a textured braid that resembles the spinal column. The tying sequence differs slightly as it is the loop that is pulled through rather than the end of the cord.

1 To make a slip knot to start, make a clockwise loop with the starting end on the left. Make a U-shaped bend with the right-hand working cord and insert into the loop. Pull the ends to tighten.

2 Tuck the working end into the loop of the slip knot leaving a larger loop to the right side and tighten the slip knot.

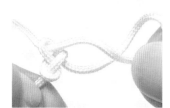

3 Twist the working end side of the larger loop forwards to create a figure of eight.

4 Pull a U-shaped bend in the working cord through the end loop on the figure of eight. Firm up the knot so far.

5 Repeat steps 2–4 until the braid is the length required, pulling the last loop all the way through the figure of eight loop.

Beads can be added so that they sit on the front of the twisted loop, or before you thread the working end into the previous loop. For more beading ideas, see Beaded Knotted Braids.

Bugle knot

A strong decorative knot, the bugle knot is traditionally used to make straps
for musical instruments and to decorate military garments.

1 Fold the cord to make a U-shaped
bend so that there is a 20cm (8in)
starting end at the bottom. Coil the
starting end around the working cord
twice to leave a loop on the left.

2 Tuck the starting end back through
the front of the coiled loops and then
firm up slightly.

> The tying of the bugle knot is similar
> to the caterpillar knot but you go
> through two loops rather than one,
> for a stronger, closely-woven braid.

3 Turn the knot over so that the
working (longer) end is on the
bottom. *Make a U-shaped bend
with the working end and, missing
the first coiled loop, tuck it under the
second loop.

4 Then pass the U-shaped bend through the last loop on
the left-hand side. Pull the last loop on the opposite side to
the working end to firm up the knot.

5 Repeat from * to make the braid the length required. Pull
the working end out after weaving under the two coiled
loops to secure the knot. Keep the working end at the
bottom when making the loops so that the top cords lie at
the same angle along the braid.

The reverse side of the bugle cord is quite different from
the front and looks like a plaited braid.

> Beads can be stitched into the braid or added as
> you knot – see Beaded Knotted Braids.

Ringbolt hitch viceroy

The ringbolt hitch viceroy is a variation of the ringbolt hitch, which is a knot usually worked around a pole. Both share the same attractive interwoven pattern down the front but this version is worked as a braid.

1 To make a slip knot to start, make an anticlockwise loop with the working end on the left. The starting end has to be twice the length of the braid plus approximately 15cm (6in). Make a U-shaped bend with the starting end and insert into the loop. Pull the ends to tighten.

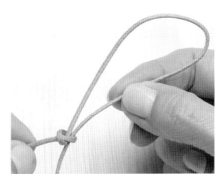

2 Pull the loop of the slip knot out to the length of the finished braid. This shortens the starting end to leave a 15cm (6in) tail.

3 Take the working end out to the right and under the long loop cord. Then bring it round and back down under itself. Pull the working end through and firm up the knot.

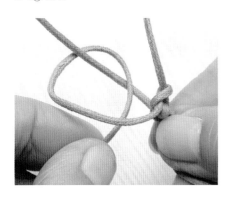

4 Take the working end out to the left and under the long loop cord, bringing it around and back down under itself. Pull the working end through and firm up the knot.

5 Repeat steps 3 and 4 until you are nearing the end of the long loop and still have about 15cm (6in) of working end cord remaining.

6 Tuck the working end through the loop at the top. Pull firmly on the starting end to firm up the knot and finish the braid.

The ringbolt hitch viceroy can easily be embellished with beads – see Beaded Knotted Braids.

Box Braids

Box braid is one of the few truly square braids when it is worked with a flat cord, such as faux suede or leather. Narrow velvet ribbon is also an alternative for a softer effect. Try the easy knot start of the basic box braid, for jewellery or accessory projects requiring long tails, or the flat end box braid for a flat square end.

Basic box braid

Although you can make the braid with a single colour, it is easier to learn the technique if you work with two colours as shown here.

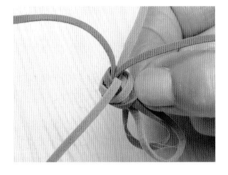

1 Fold two strands of faux suede in half and tie an overhand knot leaving long enough loops to finish the design. Splay out the four strands so that the same colours are opposite one another.

2 Lift one of the strands across the middle of the knot and the other strand of the same colour across the middle in the opposite direction.

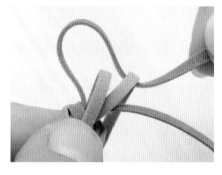

3 Hold these two strands with slight loops above the overhand knot. Pass one of the other colour strands over the first loop and under the second.

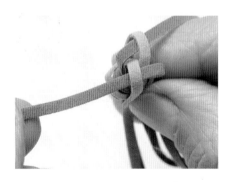

4 Repeat in the opposite direction with the other strand in the same colour, over the first and under the second loop.

5 Pull the ends to create a neat set of four squares on the top of the braid. Repeat steps 3 and 4, starting each time with loops in the colour of cord that you've just woven through.

6 When the braid is the length required you could tie the end tails with an overhand knot to match the start or glue as Flat End Box Braid, step 4.

Work with four separate pieces, each in a different colour, for interesting colour combinations.

Flat end box braid

This method of starting makes a very neat flat end to the box braid that requires no further finishing, perfect for making a key ring fob.

1 Start by crossing two different coloured cords so that the tails are all the same length. In this example the pink is on top of the green. Then as shown, fold both tails of the bottom colour (green) across the other (pink) cord leaving it fairly loose.

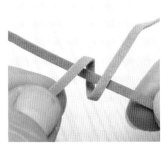

2 Take the top (pink) cord and fold it down so that it goes over, then tucks under the other colour (green) cords.

3 Take the right hand (pink) cord and pass it over, then under the other (green) colour cords in the opposite direction. Follow and repeat Basic Box Braid, steps 3–5, to make the braid.

4 To finish, apply a little jewellery glue with a cocktail stick under the loops before you pull them taut. Leave to dry, then trim neatly.

Utilitarian washers or nuts from the hardware store look fantastic added into one edge of the box braid. Finish with chain and fastenings to make an eclectic necklace. For other beading ideas see Beaded Knotted Braids.

Beaded Knotted Braids

Although knotted braids look fantastic on their own, there are times when beads can be used to enhance a design, especially for making jewellery or accessories. There are lots of different ways that you can add beads as explored here, from simply stringing beads onto the cord in between knots, to adding beads as you knot. Alternatively beads can be added after knotting, by sewing or attaching with findings.

Adding beads when tying knots

All sorts of beads can be added in with the cords as you knot, and it is the hole size not the bead size that is key, so take cord samples with you when bead shopping. In many cases it is better to add the beads onto the cord before you start knotting, rather than adding one at a time as you go.

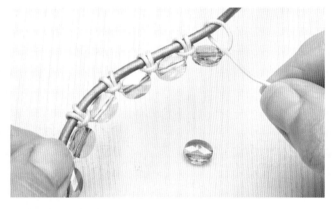

★ Individual knots like the lark's head knot can be tied one after the other around a thicker cord with beads added to the loops in between.

★ Beads can be added to the long base loop on the stitched switchback strap before you start, then the knot is tied between pairs of beads to space them evenly.

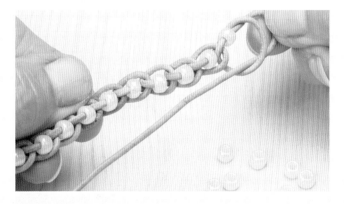

★ The caterpillar knot has a central bar inside a loop which is perfect for holding a bead. Here, a size 3 (5.5mm) pony bead has been used on a rustic 2mm leather cord.

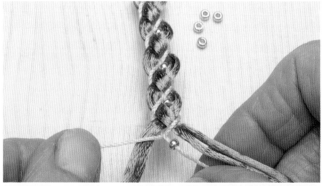

★ When tying with multiple strands, you can use a much finer cord for one or more strands to carry the beads and change the texture and look of the braid or knot. With the Celtic bar, there is a repeating cross point in the middle that is perfect for a size 6 (3.5mm) seed bead.

Sewing in individual beads

Knotted braids often have interesting textures and the little nooks and crannies can be embellished randomly or in a more regular pattern, with seed beads or other small beads.

★ The Ashoka chakra has a variety of textures within the knot. Small seed beads can be stitched into gaps or dips in the structure, and magatamas, which have a large hole, can be added around the edge as you knot to create a spiky design.

★ The zipper knot can be embellished in a several different ways as the cords criss-cross and there are pretty loops along the edge for holding beads. Here, seed beads are being stitched into the gaps to add texture and a little sparkle.

Sewing in groups of beads

As you start to work with different thicknesses and styles of cords the finished result may look quite different, and you may be inspired to embellish the knots and knotted braids with small groups of beads.

★ The snake knot has an interesting interlocking pattern that looks even better with beads added at an angle. Add the beads between the loops from top right to bottom left so that they lie neatly across the point where the two cords go under each other.

★ Braids can be embellished with seed beads to accentuate particular parts of the knotting. The ringbolt hitch viceroy, for example, has a plaited effect down the middle which looks pretty with loops of seed beads stitched along the edges.

Adding beads with findings

Jump rings and headpins can be used to attach beads and charms to almost any knot or knotted braid, to dangle from one side or around the edge, or to be added into the knot itself.

★ The looped cords of the pipa knot are perfect for adding headpin dangles to create a piece of simple jewellery. Add single beads onto headpins, make a plain loop and attach to the bottom cord.

★ Slip knot braids, such as the spinal knot or the caterpillar knot pictured, have loose loops making it easy to attach jump rings or headpin dangles. Add to both edges for a bracelet or on one side only for a necklace.

MACRAMÉ

Macramé is said to have evolved as a way to tie or create decorative fringing on rugs or woven blankets. It is one of the most versatile knotting techniques because although there are only three basic knots, these can be used singly or in unison to create a wide range of braids, flat panels or tubular structures.

Macramé Basics

Unlike other knotted braids that are usually worked in the hand, macramé is often secured to the work surface with pins or a spring clip. The square and half-knot worked with three or four cords are easy to learn, then you can move on to multistrand techniques and different ways to use the half-hitch (see Multistrand Macramé).

> ### Estimating cord lengths
> It can be difficult to work out the length of cord for working macramé if you are swapping the core and working cords around, but as a general rule the core cords are the length of the finished piece plus 15cm (6in) at each end for finishing. Allow three to four times the finished length for the working cords.

Macramé knots

There are three simple knots used in macramé, the half knot, the square knot and the half-hitch, and these can be worked in different combinations to create a variety of effects and designs. In this section how to tie the two flat knots – the half-knot and square knot is shown; for the half-hitch, which uses a different technique, see Multistrand Macramé.

Half knot

This is half a reef (square) knot (see Knotting Basics) repeated in the same direction so that the cords naturally twist. Shown here worked over two core cords, it can also be worked over one, three or more core cords.

1 Cut cords as described in estimating cord lengths and lay side by side so that the two shorter (core) cords are in the middle. *Pass the right-hand cord under the core cords and over the left-hand cord.

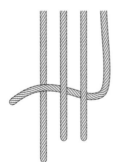

2 Take the left-hand cord over the core cords and pass it down through the loop on the right. Pull the cords to firm up the knot. Repeat from * until the spiral is the length required.

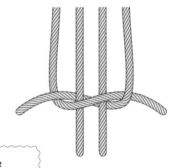

> Change the direction that you tie the knot to reverse the spiral.

Square knot

This flat knot is essentially a reef (square) * knot generally worked over two core cords, and the basic technique can be easily used to create wider panels (see Multistrand Macramé: Alternating Square Knots).

1 Arrange the cords side by side so that the two shorter (core) cords are in the middle. * Work a half knot passing the right-hand cord under the core cords and over the left-hand cord. Take the left-hand cord over the core cords and pass it down through the loop on the right.

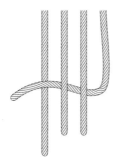

2 Reverse the process, passing the left-hand cord under the core cords and over the right-hand cord. Then take the right-hand cord and pass it down through the loop on the left. Repeat from *.

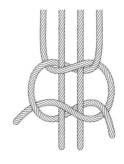

On a single square knot braid a single core cord is sufficient but not as stable as two.

Working macramé

It is best to work on a cork pin board or a sheet of foam core, so that you can use short map pins to secure the cords.

Beginning with a loop

1 Fold a length of cord in half and loop over a map pin. Secure the ends of this cord with a spring clip at the bottom of the board. Tuck a second length of cord under the core cords and tie an overhand knot (see Knotting Basics) in the middle of the working cord.

2 For a neater finish on the front side, rotate the overhand knot to the reverse, and start to tie the first macramé knot.

Beginning on a ring

Use a lark's head knot (see Knotting Basics) to attach cords to a ring, to a pendant or to a fastening ready to begin the macramé. You can add a second pair of cords, either side by side or nesting (see Nesting Lark's Head Knot). Alternatively use an overhand knot to attach a second pair of cords (see Beginning with a Loop, step 2).

For very simple braids, the cords can be taped onto a hard work surface.

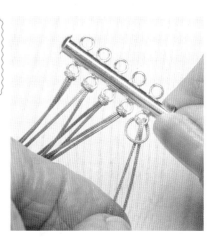

Square Knot Variations

The square knot is one of the most popular knots for making macramé bracelets and other accessories from paracord and the resulting flat knot braid is known as a Solomon bar. You can experiment with different ways of manipulating the basic square knot to make many attractive variations. While paracord is used for the samples shown, you can experiment with thicker or thinner cords to create your designs.

Crossed cords

Add a contrast cord colour to the basic square knot cords to create a cross stitch effect, with a running stitch pattern on the reverse side.

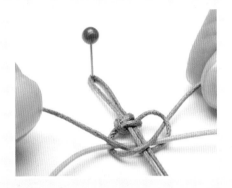

1 Start with an overhand knot and work one square knot (see Macramé Basics); before you firm up the knot, feed the ends of a contrast cord colour through the square knot under the core cords.

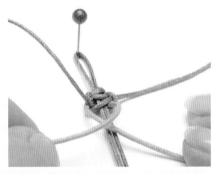

2 Cross the right-hand contrast cord over the left and drop the tails either side of the core cords.

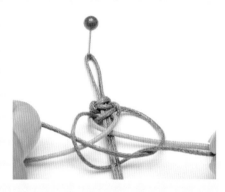

3 Work the first half of the next square knot: left-hand cord under the core cords and over the right-hand cord, right-hand cord over the core cords and down through the loop on the left.

Front: cross stitch pattern.

Reverse: running stitch pattern.

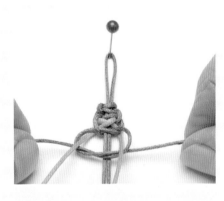

4 Lift the contrast cords up above the knots. Work the second half of the square knot, taking the right-hand cord under the contrast cords but over the core cords and the left-hand cord. Take the left-hand cord under the contrast cords but over the core cords and down through the right loop.

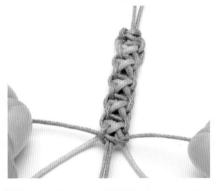

5 Repeat steps 2–4 continuing the pattern of crosses. You can cross the right cord over the left each time, or alternate for a different effect.

> To create a running stitch pattern on both sides of the braid, keep the contrast cords running down each side of the braid rather than creating a cross at step 2.

Woven square knot

Worked over the basic four strands, this produces a woven effect down the middle of the braid. Follow the step instructions carefully as the cords are not tied as a basic square knot every time.

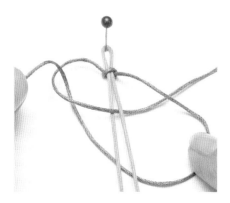

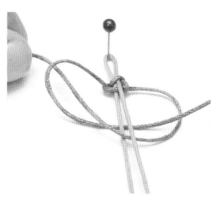

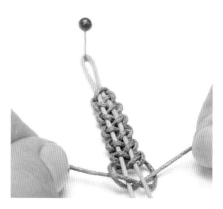

1 Tie an overhand knot and rotate it (see Beginning with a Loop, step 2). * Take the left-hand cord over the left core cord, under the right core cord, and over the right-hand cord. Pass the right-hand cord under all cords and up through the left loop as shown. Pull ends to firm up.

2 Take the right-hand cord under the right core cord, over the left core cord and under the left-hand cord. Then take the left-hand cord under all cords and up through the right loop.

3 Continue repeating from * until the braid is the length required. Work a regular square knot to finish.

Woven square knot which has an attractive picot edge and a stitched effect when worked in contrast colours.

Attach two lengths of paracord to a key ring using the lark's head knot and work one square knot. Add a contrast colour through the knot to work the crossed cords pattern. To finish work a Chinese button knot toggle at the bottom using the contrast cords (see Finishing Techniques for Knotting). Trim and seal the ends inside the toggle.

Multistrand Macramé

You can work macramé with many more cords than the basic four, to create wider bands for fringing, a belt or a cuff bracelet. Multistrand macramé can even be worked in the round to make items such as bags or plant holders. With more than four cords, however, you do need to plan ahead, working out the design, the number of cords required, and how to secure them to start.

Alternating square knots

Although you can work a square knot over a single cord (three cords in total), for alternating square knots it is better to work with multiples of four base cords.

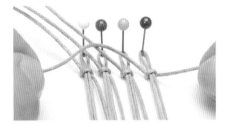

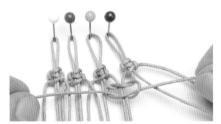

1 Set up the macramé cords – here the doubled-over cords have been pinned to a board. Tie a second cord using an overhand knot on each pair of cords and rotate for a neater finish (see Macramé Basics: Beginning with a Loop).

2 Tie a square knot (see Macramé Basics) with the first four cords, then tie a square knot with the next four cords. Work across the cords tying a square knot on each group of four cords until you reach the end of the row. Pull the knots taut so that they don't come loose.

3 On the next row, the working cords from the previous row will become the core cords and vice versa. Separate the first two cords and take these out to the right-hand side. Separate the next four cords and work a square knot.

Take care that you pick up the next four cords in order as one sometimes gets tucked behind.

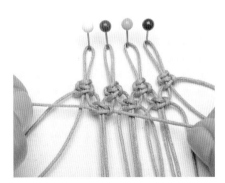

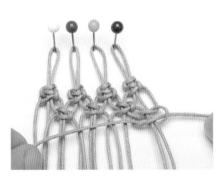

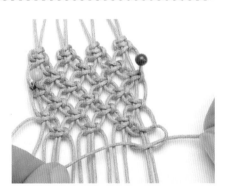

4 Work across the cords tying a square knot on each group of four cords until you reach the last two cords at the left-hand side.

5 The two spare cords are carried down to the next row. Work the next row from right to left as the first row, tying a square knot on the first four cords, and on every four cords across the row.

6 Continue to repeat the two-row tying pattern to create the macramé panel. For an even panel, try to tie knots to the same spacing each time, using pins to stabilize the panel as you work down.

Setting up to work multiple cords

Set up your cords for working by beginning with loops or by attaching the cords to a fastening, belt buckle or other fitment (see Macramé Basics). The advantage of working on a pin or foam core board is that the pins can be used to space the knots as you work, and to secure cords at an angle to make a more precise piece of knotting.

Straight half-hitch rib

Generally worked in pairs as a double half-hitch, the half-hitches are usually worked over one of the side cords to form a thick horizontal rib as shown.

1 Arrange one of the outer cords across the other cords horizontally. Bring the new outer vertical cord over the horizontal cord and back under it again to the right-hand side.

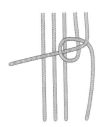

2 Take the same cord over the horizontal cord and this time bring it out to the right-hand side through the loop. Repeat the two knots using each of the vertical cords in turn to create a thick rib. When you reach the end, bring the inner cord back across the vertical cords and repeat the process in the opposite direction.

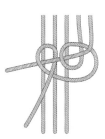

> To work the rib diagonally, see Half-hitch Variations: Diagonal Half-hitch Knots.

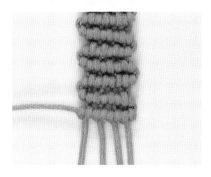

Angled-edge half-hitch rib

Half-hitches are often used to make panels with shaped sides. To work straight half-hitch, one side cord is taken back and forwards, but if you use successive cords on a particular side the edge will be angled instead.

1 Pin the right-hand cord across the other vertical cords. Work one row of half-hitch rib across this core cord, tying double half-hitches with each vertical cord. Pin the next right-hand cord across under the rib. Work a row of half-hitch rib over the new core cord finishing with a double half-hitch over the previous core cord on the left-hand side.

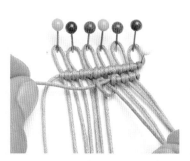

2 Pin the next right-hand cord across under the rib and work another row of half-hitches – already the panel has begun to shape diagonally. Do remember to work half-hitches over the previous core cord at the end of each row.

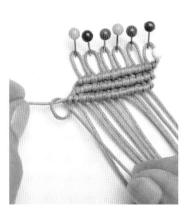

3 To change the direction to create a piece of macramé that zigzags, take the current core cord and pin it back across the vertical cords towards the right-hand side. Repeat steps 1 and 2, but now taking the next left-hand cord across to work each row.

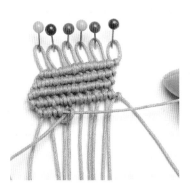

Half-hitch Variations

Half-hitch ribs can be worked at an angle for a diagonal pattern, and they can even be used to create shapes such as leaves and petals. While most macramé techniques use the double half-hitch, it is possible to create knotted designs using single half-hitches too (see Endless Falls).

Diagonal half-hitch

When making a horizontal rib the core cord is pinned straight across, but if the core cord is pinned at an angle, a diagonal rib will be created.

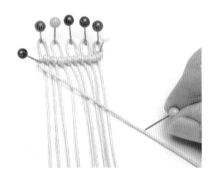 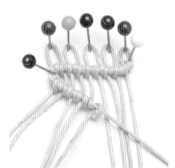 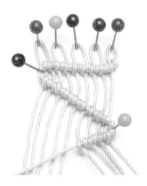 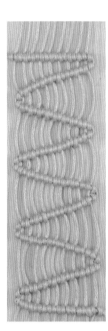

1 Work one row of half-hitch rib across the cords. Insert a pin at the end of the rib. Wrap the side (core) cord around the pin and across the vertical cord at the angle you want to create. Insert a pin to secure the core cord.

2 Tie two half-hitches with each vertical cord in turn making sure you keep the diagonal line of the rib as you firm up the knots. Make sure the vertical cords above the diagonal rib are not too loose or tight, and are lying flat.

3 To create a zigzag simply pin the core cord diagonally in the opposite direction and work half-hitches with all the vertical cords again. At the end of the row go back in the opposite direction once more, using the same core cord.

Petal shapes

With a little forward planning, it is possible to create all sorts of simple shapes with half-hitch ribs. Here the angle of the rib and the spacing has created a petal shape – use the technique to try out other patterns.

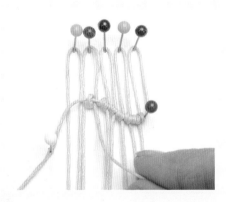 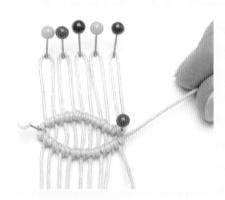

1 Pin the right-hand core cord, then take it across the vertical cords and pin so that there is a slight upwards curve on the core cord. Work half-hitches along the cord adjusting each knot to maintain the curve.

2 Bend the core cord on the left around a pin and across the vertical cords in a downwards curve to make the petal shape. Tie half-hitches over the core cord to complete the petal shape.

Half-hitches are very sculptural, so the technique lends itself to quite structured jewellery pieces. Sections of this exquisite piece of macramé with added beads could be worked as a pendant or a necklace, but worked in this way over a metal rod it makes a stunning brooch or hair clasp. For step-by-step instructions for making the Macramé Brooch, see Projects.

Endless falls

The first of the single half-hitch variations is so named because it has the appearance of a waterfall, and the vertical cords seem to flow over and tumble down behind horizontal crossed cords.

1 Fold one cord in half around a pin, with the U-shaped bend at the top. Lay the second cord behind, and working from its mid-point, cross the ends over, left first, then right, so that they overlap.

2 Bring the vertical (blue) cords up one at a time to tie a half-hitch knot behind the crossed-over (beige) cords so that the tails finish facing down in between the knots.

3 Repeat the crossing of cords and tying of half-hitches until the braid is the length required. Pull the crossed cords gently to firm up the half-hitches.

Side-by-side endless falls

For this variation of endless falls, the two cord colours are tied together in a slightly different way to create a bold stripe along the length.

1 Make a loop in the middle of one (blue) cord so that the right-hand end is over the left. Lay the second (beige) cord across the loop above the cross point.

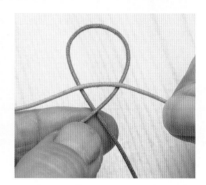

2 Wrap the right-hand end of the loop (blue) cord around the loop and then bring out through the new formed loop on the right, trapping the second (beige) cord. Pull the first (blue) cord to firm up the slip knot and arrange the cord colours alternately.

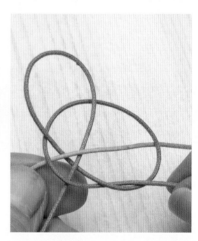

3 Work as for Endless Falls so that the vertical colours are different on each side of the braid. The crossing cords will swap from side to side.

To make a quick and easy bracelet, adjust the loop at the top of the macramé so that it is the right size for a toggle or button fastening loop.

Chain-link endless falls

A different texture and pattern can be created with the endless falls technique when four or more vertical cords are used – always work with an even number of cords.

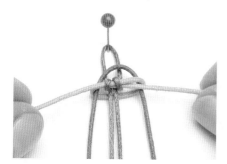 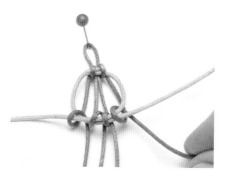 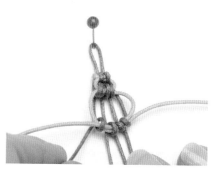

1 Start by working steps 1 and 2 of Endless Falls. Feed a third (brown) cord over the two half-hitches and down through each side of the crossed over horizontal (beige) cords. Pull the crossed cords to firm up the knot.

2 Cross the horizontal (beige) cords again, right over left. Work half-hitches with all four vertical cords, taking each cord down on the right-hand side of the half-hitch. Pull the horizontal side cords to firm up the knot.

3 Repeat step 2, but this time take the vertical cords down on the left-hand side of each half-hitch. Continue repeating these two rows until the braid is the length required, reducing back to two half-hitches at the end.

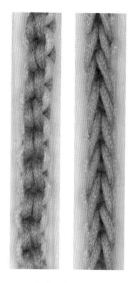 

Endless falls, front side, which looks like a waterfall, and the reverse side, which has an attractive chevron pattern down the length.

Chain-link endless falls, front side with its ribbed effect, and the reverse side, which looks like a chain-linked watchstrap.

As the endless falls technique is tied with simple knots, it can be worked in chunky paracord to make a more masculine bracelet or with finer cords for a dainty design. To embellish with beads, add a bead at either side before you cross the cords. For more embellishing ideas, see Adding Beads to Macramé.

Adding Beads to Macramé

While macramé is an attractive knotting technique unadorned, it can be embellished easily with beads and gems to create different styles. Shamballa-style bracelets with sparkly beads added into a single row of square knots is one of the most popular techniques for embellished macramé.

Selecting beads and cords

Beads of all shapes and sizes can be added to macramé as you work just so long as the cord can fit through the bead hole. The size of bead and cord you choose will depend on whether you want to create a chunky design or a piece of micro macramé, but whichever effect you are going for, the techniques you use will be the same.

Adding beads to core cords

It is easier to string all the beads onto the core cords at once rather than adding the beads one at a time as you need them.

1 Depending on the size of the bead hole, work the first section of macramé over single or double core cords. Add the bead, then secure the cord at the bottom of the board with a spring clip.

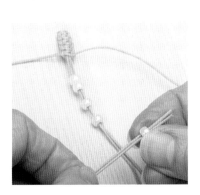

2 Push the first bead up to the last knot. Bring the working cords down either side of the bead and work a square knot beneath. You can work one or more square knots between the beads.

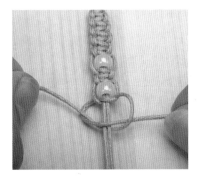

3 If working half-hitches, continue working the knots until the macramé twists around to bring the working cords back out at the sides before adding a bead.

Adding beads to working cords

When adding beads to the working cords, the beads can be smaller as there is only a single strand of cord to pass them through.

1 Beads are added as you work, so adding only the beads you require to each working cord, push them up to the previous knot.

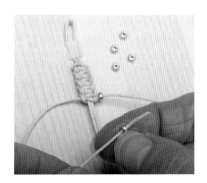

2 Work the next macramé knot around the core cords as before. Continue adding beads on the outer working cords after every knot.

On a wider band of macramé, the outer working cords are carried down to the next row of knots. You can add a bead onto each of these cords to create an attractive edging.

Adding rhinestones

Rhinestone or diamanté cup chain, a snake-like strip of small crystals in settings linked with short bars, is generally used to make exotic costume jewellery as it imitates more expensive diamonds.

1 Using 1mm cord, secure two shorter strands for the core cords and two longer strands for the working cords. Work a section of macramé with square knots (see Macramé Knots: Square Knots). Lay the rhinestone cup chain on top of the core cords.

2 Work the first half of the square knot, left-hand cord under the core cords and the chain, then over the right-hand cord. Pull the cords up so that the knot lies between the first two rhinestones.

3 Work the second half of the square knot, right-hand cord under the core cords and the chain, then over the left-hand cord, and pull up so that this knot also lies between the first two rhinestones.

4 Repeat steps 2 and 3 to work a square knot between each of the rhinestones until you have completed the length of the chain. Work a section of unembellished square knot macramé to finish.

> Use wire cutters to cut the rhinestone cup chain, stretching the chain and trimming it so that the metal lug is cut flush with the next setting.

Incorporate beads or rhinestone cup chain into a simple square knot braid to make these delightful, brightly coloured bracelets. The clever design starts with a cord loop, then the tails are used to tie a pretty Chinese button knot for a toggle. For step-by-step instructions for making the Rhinestone Bracelets, see Projects.

Finishing Techniques for Knotting

The starting of macramé and other knotting techniques is often secured with a loop or onto a fastening, so that there are no raw ends. The working end, however, always has ends to finish. You can simply leave a fringe if the design allows, or use one of several finishing techniques.

Gluing the ends

Some glues dry out and become brittle but jewellery glue such as E6000 or G-S Hypo Cement, will stay pliable once dry for a more secure and lasting join.

1 Use a cocktail stick or a glue tube with a fine nozzle to apply a little glue under the end cords where they emerge from the last knot. Leave for 24 hours to dry.

> Do not use instant superglue or gel (cyanoacrylate) as these may go hard and crack over time.

2 Check that the cord ends are secure. For wax cotton cords trim close to the knot.

3 If using a nylon cord, such as Chinese knotting cord, trim a little further away and then carefully melt the end with a small flame.

Tying knots

Sometimes a simple overhand knot is enough to neaten cord ends, or you could try the larger and more decorative double version.

Overhand knot

1 Tying an overhand knot (see Knotting Basics) on the end of a cord will prevent it from further fraying and neaten the end. Adding a bead before working the knot creates a more decorative finish.

Double overhand knot

1 Begin by tying an overhand knot, then take the working end through the loop a second time.

2 Pull both ends to firm up the knot, repositioning as you tighten if necessary. Add a drop of glue (see Gluing the Ends) and trim.

Cord fastenings

A fastening can be made using the macramé or knotting cords, from a simple sliding fastening with overhand knots to the more ornate Chinese button knot sliding fastening with its toggle-and-loop.

Sliding knot fastening

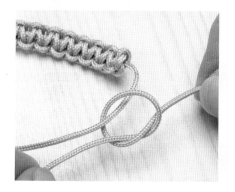

1 To make a simple slide fastening, lay the cord of the bracelet parallel, but in opposite directions. Tie an overhand knot with one end over the other cord.

2 Repeat to tie an overhand knot at the other end. Pull the knots fairly taut but not so tight that the cords can't move. Pull the tails to open and the main cords to close.

For ways to use findings to attach metal fastenings, see Finishing Techniques for Braiding.

Chinese button knot toggle fastening

1 Work to the length of braid required allowing for the toggle-and-loop fastening. Tie both core cords together in an overhand knot close to the knotting, add a touch of glue and trim the ends.

2 Using one of the side cords begin to tie a button knot around the core cords to make a toggle (see Individual Knots: Sliding Button Knot Fastening).

3 Weave the other side cord around the toggle shape to create a double strand knot. Bring both side cords up out at the top of the knot before firming up.

4 Pull the loops one at a time and work around to firm up the knot so that it finishes up around the overhand knot, next to the end of the knotting. Apply a tiny amount of glue where the cords emerge, then either trim or melt to finish, shaping the ball so that the ends are hidden.

BRAIDING

Braiding is the interweaving of strands of cord or thread, manipulating all the cords at once in a particular sequence of movements. Making braids can be as easy as a simple three-strand plait, to more challenging intricate designs made from combining eight, 16, or even more threads with Kumihimo, a Japanese braiding technique.

Plaiting and Kumihimo are the two braiding techniques explored in this section. As no special equipment is required, you can begin plaiting straight away, but the ready availability of inexpensive disks and plates makes Kumihimo very accessible too. The Kumihimo chapter begins by introducing you to all the equipment you are likely to need for this rewarding craft.

Each of the plaiting and Kumihimo techniques featured is clearly explained with fully illustrated step-by-step instruction, and while the technique samples use mainly standard cords, such as satin cord, wax cotton or leather thong, so the braiding can be clearly seen, you can experiment with all sorts of textiles like ribbons, textured yarns and even wire. There is a wide variety of different threads, cords and ribbons readily available making it possible to create an amazing array of braids for all sorts of jewellery, accessories and home-style projects, as can be seen from the many ideas included.

When experimenting with your selected strands, don't be afraid to try different thicknesses too as the change in size – going smaller as well as larger – can bring unexpected results. There are also bead-embellishing ideas included for plaiting and Kumihimo, as well as options for finishing your braids for the neatest results.

PLAITING

Plaiting is a braiding technique that you have probably done before, either to plait hair or to make a simple cord for a craft project. There are innumerable ways to plait and I have chosen a selection of easy techniques using three or more strands. Plaiting can be used to make jewellery and embellish accessories or home-style projects.

Three-strand plaiting

The simplest form of plaiting can be worked with a single cord for each strand or with bundles of different cords, chain and ribbon.

1 Secure three cords to the work surface using tape or a spring clip. Take the right-hand cord over the middle cord so that it is now the new middle cord.

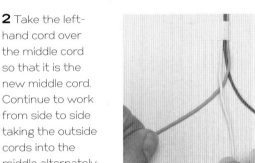

2 Take the left-hand cord over the middle cord so that it is the new middle cord. Continue to work from side to side taking the outside cords into the middle alternately.

3 Keep the tension on the cords so that the plait is close woven and even. Continue until the strand is the length required.

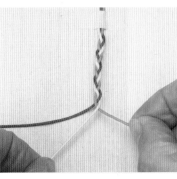

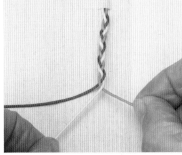

Wheat plaiting

This technique is similar to three-strand plaiting and can be worked with five, seven, or more,. always using an odd number.

1 Lay five cords together and secure to the work surface using tape or a spring clip. Take the right-hand cord over the next two cords so that there are three cords on the left and two on the right.

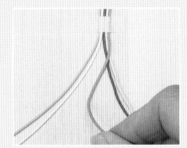

2 Take the left-hand cord over the next two cords so that there are three cords on the right and two on the left.

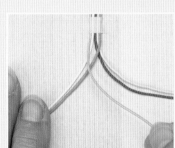

3 Continue to work from side to side taking the outside cords into the middle over two strands each time.

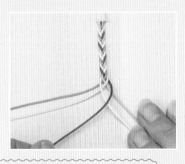

> To work with seven cords, take the outside cord over three strands each time; to work with nine cords, take the outside cord over four strands, and so on.

Basic three-strand plaiting is used to transform an eclectic mix of chain, beads and fabric into a stunning plaited necklace. For step-by-step instructions for making the Plaited Silk and Pearl Necklace, see Projects.

Flat braid plaiting technique 1

This is the easiest way to make a wide band of plaiting as the technique works for any number of strands. The start is asymmetrical.

1 Secure five or more strands on the work surface using tape or a spring clip. Take the right-hand cord and weave it over and under alternately across all the other cords.

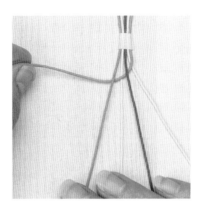

Use this technique to loosely plait strands of crocheted wire with beads to make a cuff bracelet or necklace.

2 Take the new right-hand cord and weave it over and under all the other cords including the previous cord.

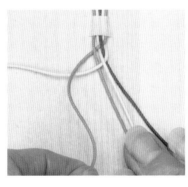

3 Continue to work in this way, always taking the next right-hand cord and weaving it across the other cords, until the plait is the length required.

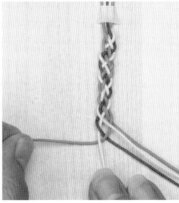

Flat braid plaiting technique 2

This technique creates a wide even plait from the start, as you work with right- and left-hand strands. It can be worked with both odd and even numbers of strands.

1 Secure an even number of strands, in this instance six, onto the work surface using tape or a spring clip. Separate the strands into two sets of three. *Take the right-hand cord over the next cord, then under the next cord, to leave two cords on the right and four on the left.

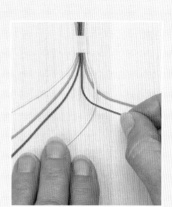

2 Take the left-hand cord under the next cord, over the next cord, then under the next cord, to leave three cords on either side again.

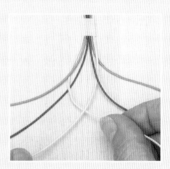

3 Repeat from * until the plait is the length you require.

To make wider plaits using an even number strands, just remember to always start with an over on the right and an under on the left.

Working with odd number of cords

For seven strands, for example, separate the cords so that there are three on the left and four on the right. Beginning with the right-hand cord, take it over, under and over to give you four cords on the left. Then take the left-hand cord over, under and over to give you four strands on the right. The same sequence is repeated at either side, and continued to make the plait the length required.

Five-strand plaiting

A variation of flat braid plaiting, this has been worked using a flatter contrast cord for the core (middle) cord. Cut the plaiting strands about 1½ times the length of the core cord.

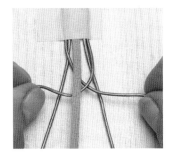
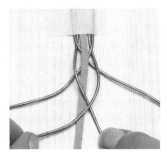

1 Tape the cords to the work surface with the flat (core) cord in the middle. Take the left-hand cord under the core cord. Pass the right-hand cord under the core cord and over the new left-hand cord, to form a cross behind the flat core.

2 Take the new left-hand cord over the other left-hand cord and over the core cord. Pass the new right-hand cord over the other two cords on the right and over the core to form a cross behind the flat core.

3 Take the new left-hand cord over the left-hand cord and under the core cord. Pass the new right-hand cord over the other two cords on the right and under the core cord as shown.

4 Repeat steps 2 and 3 until the braid is the length you require.

> Tape the other end of the flat cord before you begin to make it easier to keep a good tension with the plaiting.

Five-strand plaiting variation

To create a more distinctive cross pattern, at step 2 take the new left-hand cord **under** the other left-hand cord and **over** the core cord, then take the new right-hand cord **under** the other two cords on the right and **over** the core.

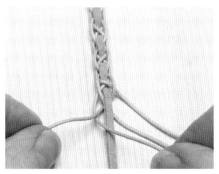

To make a chunky bracelet suitable for a teenage boy, choose six cords in grey and two cords in blue. Lay the blue cords in between pairs of grey ready to plait using the variation technique for five-strand plaiting, then add end cones and a fastening to finish (see Finishing Techniques for Braiding).

Secret plaiting

With this technique you can make a plaited belt or bracelet from a single piece of leather.

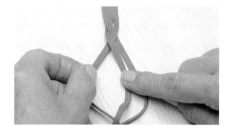

1 Cut a piece of suede or leather measuring 23 x 1.5cm (9 x 5/8in), then cut the centre section into three equal strips leaving 12mm (½in) uncut at **both** ends.

2 To make the three-strand plait (see Three-strand Plaiting), pull the right-hand cord to one side then bring the left-hand cord into the gap and lay it beside the right cord.

3 Take the right-hand cord into the gap and lay it beside the left-hand cord. Then take the left-hand cord into the gap and lay it beside the right-hand cord.

4 Bring the bottom end up and tuck it through the gap beside the left-hand cord, then straighten out.

5 There is now a gap at the bottom between the right-hand cord and two twisted left-hand cords. Take the bottom end and tuck it through this gap too. Continue plaiting right, left, right to unravel the twisted plaits at the bottom.

6 Start again from step 2 taking the left-hand cord into the gap and then left, right, left and through the gap beside the left-hand cord (to end step 4), and repeat step 5. Continue until the suede strand is evenly plaited to the end, finishing with the right, left, right to unravel.

> You can also use secret plaiting to plait bead or chain strands once the end bars have been attached.

Secret plaiting makes a quick-and-easy bracelet. Start with a strip of leather 2.5cm (1in) longer than the finished length; cut the centre section into three or six pieces using a rotary cutter and plait. Insert snap fasteners at each end to make a simple closure.

Plaiting with Beads and Chain

As with other knotting and braiding techniques, it is always exciting to find ways to incorporate beads into your plaiting. The difficulty lies in finding beads with large enough holes to suit the cord or plaiting material being used. Try these ideas, then experiment by using a thinner cord for one or more of the strands so that smaller beads can be incorporated. There are also ideas for incorporating chain into your plaiting.

Plaiting with bead strings

Seed beads sold in pre-strung hanks are perfect for plaiting. You'll find it easiest to attach the findings while the beads are straight, so the secret plaiting technique is best.

1 Choose a selection of bead strings and cut them all to the same length. Secure both ends into a suitable finding such as end caps, end bars or a slider fastening. Separate the strands into three equal bundles.

2 Use the secret plaiting technique to plait the strands, easing the clasp or end cap through the gaps carefully.

> The strings are bought to a standard length, or you can transfer the beads onto other beading cord or wire if you prefer. Allow for 5–10% shrinkage to ensure your bracelet or necklace is finished to the correct length.

Plaiting with big beads

Many larger beads have holes that are about 1mm in size, which are ideal for stringing onto leather or wax cotton cord.

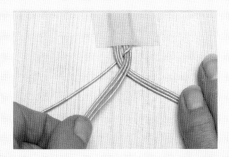

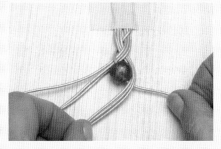

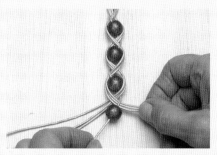

1 Cut seven strands of cord all the same length and tape to the work surface. Separate two bundles of three cords on the left leaving a single strand on the right. Work three-strand plaiting: right to the middle, left to the middle, right to the middle.

2 Pick up a bead on the single cord and continue the plaiting sequence: left to the middle, right to the middle, left to the middle.

3 Continue to pick up a bead on the single strand each time and repeat a three-move sequence of plaiting alternating sides, until the plait is the length required.

> When working a simple three-strand plait, increasing the number of strands of cord used for the unbeaded strands will balance the weight of the beads.

Two-strand plaiting with chain

This is essentially a three-strand plait as the chain is the third strand, even though it doesn't move from its position on the right.

1 Cut two bundles of thread – I used 16 lengths of stranded cotton (floss) in total – and tie together at one end with an overhand knot (see Knotting Basics), taking care to keep the thread bundles separate. Feed the right-hand length through the top chain link.

2 Plait the left-hand bundle over the right, then bring it up through the back of the same chain link.

3 Continue to take the left-hand bundle over the right and into the back of each chain link, plaiting twice into each chain link. (Or plait once only if your thread bundles are thicker.)

4 Tie the thread bundles with an overhand knot at the end to secure.

> Choose a chain with large enough links to feed the cords/threads through, and use a twisted wire needle, a simple loop of cord or even an opened paper clip to assist you.

Adding beads into chain plait

To make a micro bracelet, plait 1mm cord through chain and add size 3 (5.5mm) beads as you go. Use two strands of cord folded in half to create the toggle loop.

1 Cut two cords about 60cm (24in) long, fold in half and tie an overhand knot near the top to make a toggle loop. Take the left-hand cord up through the first chain link and the next cord up through the second link.

2 Put the right-hand cord out of the way. Plait the left-hand cord over the middle cord and the right-hand cord into the middle (see Three-strand Plaiting).

3 Add a bead to the middle cord and take it up through the next chain link. Plait again, left into the middle, right into the middle.

4 Repeat from step 3 to the end of the chain pulling the cords taut so that the beads are sitting on the loops at the outside.

5 Either trim the spare cord off or feed the spare cord down through the beads to stabilize the beaded plait. Work a button knot at the end (see Finishing Techniques for Knotting).

Embroidery thread is perfect for plaiting into chain as you can select the exact number or strands suitable for the size of the chain links. This necklace uses cotton perlé with organza ribbon to soften the effect of the chain, for pleasing contrasting textures. For step-by-step instructions for making the Chain Plait Necklace, see Projects.

KUMIHIMO

Kumihimo is a braiding technique originating from Japan – the name means 'gathered threads' in Japanese – and it is traditionally worked on wooden stool-shaped structures called Marudai, which are beautiful but expensive. Kumihimo disks and plates made from a lightweight dense foam are more affordable for beginners and occasional users, and can be used to make a wide variety of different-shaped braids using one or more of six basic moves that either pass the cords over the centre hole or around the edge of the disk or plate.

Equipment and Materials

Traditionally Kumihimo braids were made on a Marudai and worked with bundles of fine silk threads to make an obi-jime, the belt worn around a kimono. Contemporary braiders can choose instead to work Kumihimo using the versatile and very portable disk or plate, using a variety of readily available cords, threads or even wire.

Kumihimo tools

It is essential to have a disk or Marudai to work Kumihimo, so review the options and decide whether you want to go down the traditional route or to start simply with a disk or plate.

Disk and plate

These simple tools are made from dense foam with numbered slots for the cords or thread (see Setting Up the Disk or Plate). The disks have slots all round with numbers from 1 to 32 (the number refers to the slot on the left as you move clockwise). The square plates have numbers along the top and bottom edges, distinguished either with a circle on the bottom row or a different set of numbers. There are letters down each side either with lower case and capitals or a circle on one set. The round disk can be used for both round and flat braids but you may find it easier to use the square plate for flat braids as it has a rectangular hole in the middle.

Marudai

Unlike the Kumihimo disk or plate, the Marudai (round stand) has no numbers to guide you or slots to secure the cords or threads. It is still the same basic technique but you do need more equipment to get started. It is essential to create a balance between the cords and braid using weighted bobbins and counterweights (see Setting Up the Marudai). You are not restricted to a particular number of slots with a Marudai and, as it is free-standing, the braid is worked with two hands, making it a very relaxing and rhythmic way to work Kumihimo.

> Traditionally flat woven braids are worked on a Takadai, which is the flat braid version of a Marudai but with a much larger more cumbersome frame.

Bobbins

It is fairly easy to work Kumihimo braids with cords up to about 75cm (30in), but when working with longer cords, you will find it much easier to wind the cord onto little bobbins. You can use cotton reels or even a piece of folded card, but these specially designed bobbins are inexpensive with a stopping mechanism inbuilt to secure the cords. Marudai bobbins are available in a range of different weights.

Wire for Kumihimo

Wire can be used for any Kumihimo braid provided that it is soft enough or thin enough to be manipulated successfully. It has to withstand being bent back and forwards without breaking or becoming harder. For more information, see Essential Equipment: Wire.

What wire?

Wire is available in a range of cross sections but round is generally the most successful for Kumihimo; 0.315mm (30swg) cut into bundles of four strands is a good way to start. You can incorporate wire into bundles of thread to make a braid that will hold its shape when bent or add beads to thicker wire to make beaded bangles.

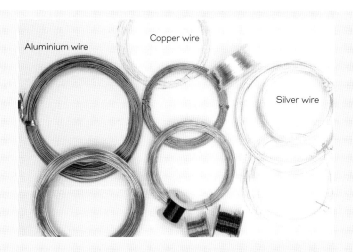

Copper or copper-core wires
Craft jewellery wire is ideal for Kumihimo braiding.

Aluminium wires
As these are very soft, you could use a thicker diameter, but take care as they can be brittle if overworked.

Silver wire
That sold as soft condition is suitable for braiding.

Weights

Weights are traditionally used with the Marudai to counterbalance the weight of the bobbins (see Setting Up the Marudai); the centre-weight, which can be a bag filled with coins, should be equal to half the combined weight of the bobbins. The Kumihimo disk and plate have slots and so it is not necessary to use a weight as the slots keep the cords or threads in place, but I have found that round braids in particular are smoother and more even when a centre-weight of about 70–100g (2½– 3½oz) is used (thicker cords will need a slightly heavier weight than thinner cords).

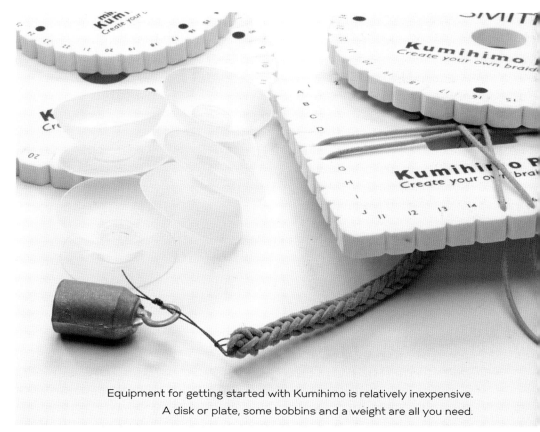

Equipment for getting started with Kumihimo is relatively inexpensive. A disk or plate, some bobbins and a weight are all you need.

Cords and threads for Kumihimo

Kumihimo can be worked using any material that can be bent and manipulated into a braid. Traditionally fine silk cords are used but there are many more options. For more information, see Essential Equipment: Cords and Threads.

Thick or thin?

Japanese braiders use bundles of fine silk thread to work Kumihimo. Typically each bundle has 40 threads and so, although the thread is fine like a sewing thread, the bundles themselves are quite thick. To work traditionally, silk or imitation silk threads such as Shinon or Biron can be bought pre-cut in lengths approximately 3m (3yd) long. But there are many more options available to you,

from a fine embroidery thread to a thick rattail or leather cord. You can also combine different thicknesses of cord or thread in the same braid to create different textures or to add beads (see Beaded Kumihimo Braids). There is no particular restriction on thread/cord size when using a Marudai, but with the disk or plate they have to be thin enough to fit into the slots.

Silk thread Group in bundles for strong braids that have a fabulous sheen; silk embroidery thread is also suitable.

Satin cord A beautiful cord with a high sheen ideal for Kumihimo and available in a range of thicknesses.

Chinese knotting cord Suitable for making textured braids, this round cord has a centre core so stays round when braided.

Superlon™ This twisted nylon cord makes stiff Kumihimo braids, and is perfect for adding beads or working around a core. You can make a fine braid using Superlon™ cord only or mix it with other cords such as rattail to create different textures.

Embroidery threads The subtle sheen of stranded cotton (floss) and cotton perlé for example, produce a matte finish on braids; metallic embroidery threads add a touch of sparkle.

Ribbons and flat braids Ideal to bring a change of texture to your Kumihimo braids; look out for tubular mesh ribbons, either synthetic or metal.

> Ribbon works particularly well for techniques where some cords are not braided every time, to give you longer strands on the outside of the braid (see Honeycomb Braid).

Preparing to Braid

Kumihimo braids can be worked on a traditional Marudai or the round disk. A square plate is also available to make it easier to work flat braids (see Flat Braids). Before beginning braiding there are a few things to familiarize yourself with, from cutting your cord lengths to setting up threads on your disk or plate, as well as how to interpret the Quick Guide information which accompanies the featured techniques.

Setting up the disk or plate

Before you can start braiding, you need to set up the disk or plate with the threads required. The layout of cords is described as being in a particular slot or as being at the top, bottom, left side or right side.

Make your own disk or plate
You can buy a disk or plate (see Suppliers) or to get started straight away, copy the disk and plate templates (see Templates) onto a stiff card such as grey board. Carefully cut out, snip into the slots, then cut out the hole in the middle.

1 Prepare the cords with a lark's head knot or overhand knot depending on whether you are working with an even or odd number of threads (see Preparing the Braiding Threads) and tuck down through the centre hole in the disk/plate. Keeping the knot in the middle of the centre hole, arrange the cords as shown on the quick guide photo or diagram for your chosen technique (see Working from the Quick Guides), tucking them into the appropriate slots.

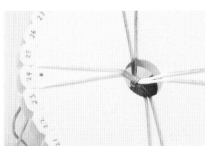

2 For a first project it is easier to have two colours arranged in groups rather than the same colour for all strands. Make sure the cords are taut but that the knot in the middle is below the top surface of the disk/plate.

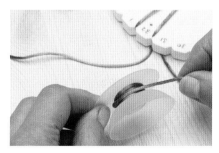

3 If the cords are more than 75cm (30in) long, wind the excess yarn onto bobbins. Lightweight bobbins are perfect for working on the disk or plate.

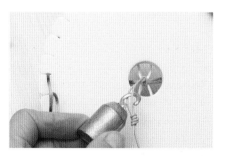

4 If you prefer to, you can add a centre-weight to the knot on the cords. It is not essential but I find using a weight 70–100g (2½–3½oz) with the disk in particular makes round braids smoother and more even.

Setting up the Marudai

The top surface of the Marudai is known as the mirror because it 'reflects what is down below', in other words the beauty of the braided cord. The Marudai itself can be made from wood, plastic or clear acrylic.

There are no slots or numbers on the Marudai, instead the cords/threads are draped over the top surface and down through the hole in the centre. As it is free-standing you can use both hands to move two cords at the same time. Traditionally the cords/threads are tied at one end with an overhand knot, held temporarily in place under the mirror, by threading a chopstick through the middle of the bundle. You can then separate the cords/threads into the right number of bundles and wind the ends onto weighted bobbins. These are counter-balanced by attaching a centre-weight equivalent to half the combined weight of the bobbins. A heavier centre-weight will make a looser braid.

Use a lark's head loop to hang the weight bag. As you work the braid slide the lark's head up to a new position near the top surface.

Preparing the braiding threads

When working out the length of the strands, much will depend on the thickness, but as a general rule the cords or threads used for Kumihimo should be twice the length of the finished braid plus 15cm (6in) to allow for the width of the disk or plate.

It is almost impossible to join in other lengths of cord during braiding so always make sure you have plenty to start. Depending on the colour sequence in the braiding you can cut the strands as double length or single length.

For an even number of strands

If there is an even number of strands or bundles of each colour, cut double the length required and use a lark's head knot (see Knotting Basics) to secure the mid-point.

For an odd number of strands

For an odd number of different colour strands, tie the cords together before you start with an overhand knot (see Knotting Basics).

Working from the Quick Guides

These contain all the information needed to create a particular braid, from the starting positions of threads to finished sample.

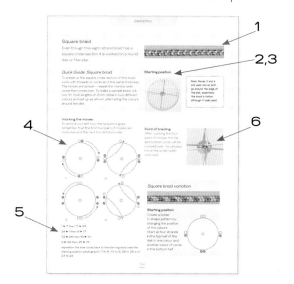

1 Finished sample

Each technique has a finished sample to show what that particular arrangement of colours and thickness of cords looks like when braided. To create the same pattern you need to choose either exactly the same colours or a new selection of colours with similar hues so that your braid has a similar balance.

2, 3 Starting position

It is essential to get the correct colours of cords in the right position to start. One of two visuals is provided for the starting position, either a photograph (2) to show the slot numbers and colours of the starting position on the disk (or plate) or (3) a diagram without numbers which shows the cord positions on the Marudai. The dots on the starting diagram (which represent the threads/cords used) will vary in colour and size so that when you are adding texture or beads you'll be able so see at a glance where the different thickness of cords are placed to start.

> Many of the braids have a pattern such as a spiral or stripe that only works if colours are in a particular position.

4 Working the moves diagrams

Step diagrams are provided for the sequence of thread moves, shown by the arrowed lines indicating where threads start and where they are moved to. When working on the Marudai, the moves diagrams are enough to guide you through the thread moves, but

when working on the disk, you should also refer to the moves abbreviated list (see 5). In the diagram caption, I refer to the cord positions as top, bottom, left and right. Note that sometimes the disk rotates as you work the braid so top is not always at 32/1 but refers to the position of the cords at that particular time and position in the sequence.

5 Working the moves abbreviated list

This is provided to be used alongside the moves diagrams as a written record of the order of the thread moves. I find that when using a disk, it is better to follow the written moves but to look at the Marudai diagram as you go to see which direction to move in. This gives you the confidence that you are placing the cords in the right slots, but allows you to see at a glance the pattern of moves so you get into a rhythm very quickly.

6 Point of braiding

A close up photograph shows the braid at the end of the sequence of moves outlined in 4 and 5, so that you can check that the moves have been executed correctly before starting the moves sequence again. If you have made a mistake, go back and rearrange the cords in the correct position before continuing.

Repositioning threads

When working some of the braids on a disk or plate you will need to move cords back to the start position after completing part or all of the sequence of moves. This is called repositioning and is necessary because there is a limited number of slots.

It is possible when working on a disk to swap the cords without needing to reposition – hold the first cord after one move beside the correct slot with your thumb and then pull it into the vacant slot once you take the other cord over to the opposite side.

Finishing the braids

Once the braid is complete it can be removed from the Marudai, disk or plate. To prevent the braid unravelling, tie a loose overhand knot (see Knotting Basics) or wrap a short length of wire around the cords to secure. You can then select one of the finishing techniques (see Finishing Techniques for Braiding).

Basic Moves

All Kumihimo braids are created with a series of moves, and how the cords are positioned and moved makes a specific braid. There are hundreds of possible braid designs, but they are all made using one or more of just six basic moves. Essentially you either move the cords across the centre of the disk or Marudai, or around the edge, or you cross the cords over. Apart from the woven flat braid, all the braids in this book use these moves, although the flat braids are best worked on the square plate. Try out the moves to become familiar with the techniques and the diagrams.

Cords going across the centre

When moves are made across the centre of the Marudai or disk/plate, a solid braid will be produced.

Basic move 1

The cords gradually move around the disk and so it is better to disregard the numbers and concentrate on the moves. One cord moves down and another moves up passing across the centre of the disk: top right to bottom right, bottom left to top left. After the move there are the same number of cords in each section as before.

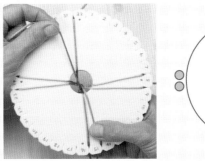 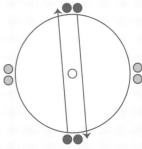

1 ➤ 15 then 17 ➤ 31

In the photograph, the first move, top right to bottom right, has been completed leaving only one cord at the top and three at the bottom. Now move the cord at bottom left up to top left so that there are two cords top and bottom again.

Basic move 2

Four cords change places across the centre of the disk. When working on a disk or plate the cords need to be spaced at the top as shown to allow the cords to move into the gap: two bottom cords up, two top cords down. After the move there are the same number of cords in each section as before.

 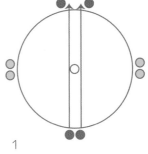 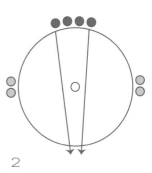

1   2

16 ➤ 1 then 17 ➤ 32
2 ➤ 16 then 31 ➤ 17

In the photograph, the first pair of moves, two bottom cords to top, has been completed, leaving no cords at the bottom, and now the two outer top cords are to be moved to the slots at the bottom.

Cords going around the outer edge

If all moves are made around the edge, the braid made will be hollow. See also Cords Crossing Over.

Basic move 3

Two cords move around the outer edge, from one part of the disk to another. The cords don't cross over the centre or any other cords: top to the right, bottom to the left. After the move there is only one cord top and bottom and three cords on each side.

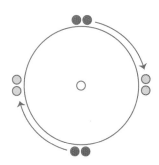

1 ➤ 7 then 17 ➤ 23

In the photograph, the first move, top right to side right, has been completed leaving only one cord at the top and three at the right side. Now move the cord at bottom left up to side left so that there are three cords on each side and one cord top and bottom.

Cords crossing over

These moves are made around the edge, but also cross over one or more stationary cords.

Basic move 4

Two cords move around the outer edge, from one part of the disk to another. Each cord goes in a different direction crossing over one stationary cord as it moves. The cords do not pass over the centre: left top over one cord and around to the right, bottom right over one cord and around to the left. After the move there is only one cord top and bottom and three cords on each side.

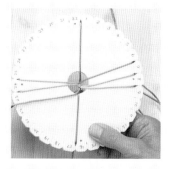
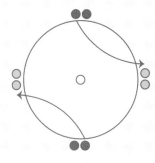

32 ➤ 7 then 16 ➤ 23

In the photograph, the first move, top left to side right, has been completed leaving only one cord at the top and three at the bottom. Now move the cord at bottom right up to side left so that there is only one cord top and bottom and three cords on each side.

All working the moves diagrams can be used for disks/ plates and the Marudai because the moves are essentially the same. However, when using a Marudai you are hands-free, enabling you to move two cords at once, but as you have to hold the disk and plate in one of your hands, you can only move one thread at a time.

Basic move 5

Cords move around the outer edge crossing over two stationary cords. The cords do not pass over the centre but there needs to be a gap between the side cords so that the moving cord has a vacant slot: top left to middle right, bottom right to middle left. After the move there is only one cord top and bottom and three cords on each side.

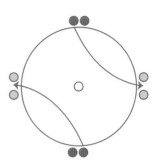

32 ➤ 8 then 16 ➤ 25

In the photograph, the first move, top left to the middle slot side right, has been completed leaving only one cord at the top and three at the right side. Now move the cord at bottom right up to middle slot side left so that there is only one cord top and bottom and three cords on each side.

Basic move 6

Two cords from one side cross over as they move around the outer edge. Each cord also goes over two stationary cords. The cords do not pass over the centre. Usually the right cord is moved first so that the left cord finishes on top of the right: bottom right to left side top, bottom left to right side top. After the move there are no cords on the bottom, three cords on each side and two at the top.

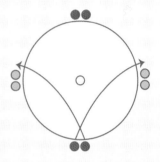

17 ➤ 7 then 16 ➤ 26

In the photograph, the first move, bottom left to top side right, has been completed leaving only one cord at the bottom and three at the right side. Now move the cord at bottom right up to top side left so that there are no cords at the bottom and three cords on each side.

Detail from the Square Braid Necklace (see Projects): the square braid is just one of the braids made using Basic Move 6 in combination with Basic Move 3. Depending on the cord colours used and their start position, a variety of patterns can be created.

Round Braids

These are the most popular of the Kumihimo braids, and perhaps most popular of all is the basic round braid 1, but as you will find out there is a wide variety of round braids and it's great fun trying out the different styles. You can work all the round braids on either a disk or a Marudai and because Kumihimo is such a versatile technique, enjoy experimenting with different colours and textures of thread, ribbons or cords to make your own unique braids.

Round braid 1

This easy eight-strand round braid is worked by repeating one move – Basic Move 1 – over and over.

Starting position

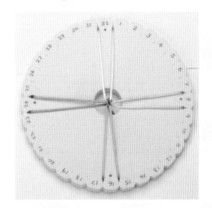

To make a sample 20cm (8in) braid, cut four 1m (1yd) lengths of 2mm rattail in different colours and set up as in the starting position.

Quick Guide: Round braid 1

Set up cords in the starting position then work the sequence as shown in the diagrams. On a disk this braid is usually worked by rotating the disk a quarter turn to the left after each pair of moves so that the next set of cords to be moved are top and bottom of the disk, essentially repeating diagram 1 each time. The cords will progress around the disk, so after the first four pairs of moves it is better to ignore the numbers and repeat working the move diagram 1 from then on.

Working the moves

Rotate disk to the left (anticlockwise) after each pair of moves. After two pairs of moves the colours are back in pairs, after eight pairs of moves they are back at the original start position.

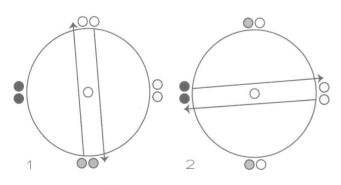

1 ➤ 15 then 17 ➤ 31

9 ➤ 23 then 25 ➤ 7

16 ➤ 30 then 32 ➤ 14

24 ➤ 6 then 8 ➤ 22

Point of braiding

After making the four pairs of moves the cords are still in a right-angle cross shape but they have been moved around to the next pair of slots in each quarter.

Round braid 1 variation

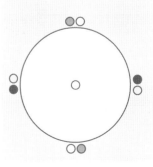

Starting position

For a mottled pattern. start with two different colours in each quarter of the disk.

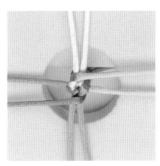

Z and S spirals

This variation of round braid 1 produces a distinctive spiral down the length of the braid and you can create a spiral that coils round to the left like an S or one that coils to the right like a Z.

Starting position

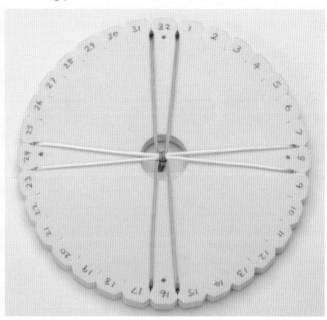

Quick Guide: Spiral braid

Set up cords in the starting position then work the sequence as shown. If you rotate the disk a quarter turn to the left (anticlockwise) after each pair of moves you will get a Z spiral or turn the disk a quarter turn to the right (clockwise) after each pair of moves for the S spiral. The cords will progress around the disk, so after the first four pairs of moves it is better to ignore the numbers and repeat the sequence of moves as shown.

To make a sample braid, use two 1m (1yd) lengths of rattail in two contrasting colours and set up as shown. The starting position is the same for both spirals and so you can make a 10cm (4in) sample of each, reversing the spiral (see Reversing the Spiral).

Working the moves for Z spiral

Turn the disk a quarter turn to the left after each pair of moves. As the cords move around the slots just repeat: top right to bottom right, bottom left to top left, then rotate the disk a quarter turn to the left.

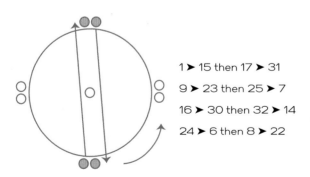

1 ➤ 15 then 17 ➤ 31
9 ➤ 23 then 25 ➤ 7
16 ➤ 30 then 32 ➤ 14
24 ➤ 6 then 8 ➤ 22

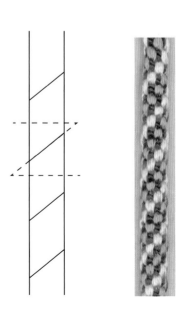

Working the moves for S spiral

Turn the disk a quarter turn to the right after each pair of moves. As the cords move around the slots just repeat: top left to bottom left, bottom right to top right, then rotate the disk a quarter turn to the right.

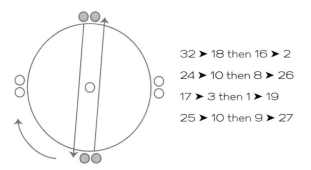

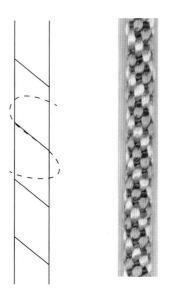

32 ➤ 18 then 16 ➤ 2
24 ➤ 10 then 8 ➤ 26
17 ➤ 3 then 1 ➤ 19
25 ➤ 10 then 9 ➤ 27

Reversing the spiral

You can combine the S and Z spirals to create a braid with a zigzag pattern down the length.

Quick Guide: Reversing the spiral

Set up cords in the starting position shown for the Z and S spirals. If you start with the cords either side of the dots on the disk you will know when to reverse the spiral. Work the sequence as shown in working the moves for Z spiral. At the end of 16 pairs of moves, when the pairs of cords are lying either side of the dots once again, you need to twist each of the pairs of cords as shown in the detail photograph and then start to work the S spiral sequence from the pair of cords to the right of the last working pair. After 16 pairs of moves, twist the cords again and start the Z spiral from the pair of cords to the right of the last working pair and so on.

> For longer gaps between zigzags, change direction after 32 pairs of moves, so cords move half way around the disk to the next dots.

When you are ready to reverse the spiral take a pair of cords out of their slots, twist the top cord over the bottom cord and replace into the slots either side of the dot. Turn the disk a quarter turn and repeat on the second pair of cords as shown; continue to turn and twist until all four pairs of cords have been twisted.

Round braid 2

This braid is worked by repeating Basic Move 1, moving opposite pairs of cords in sequence vertically, horizontally and once on each diagonal.

Quick Guide: Round braid 2

Set up cords with just one cord in each of eight slots spaced equally around the disk or Marudai as shown in the starting position, then work the sequence as shown in the diagrams. When working on a disk, move either the top cord first or the one on the right. The cords will progress around the disk, so after the first four pairs of moves it is better to ignore the numbers and just repeat the moves as shown on the diagrams.

Starting position

To make a sample braid, cut two 1m (1yd) lengths of rattail of two different colours and set up as shown with colours alternating around the disk.

Working the moves

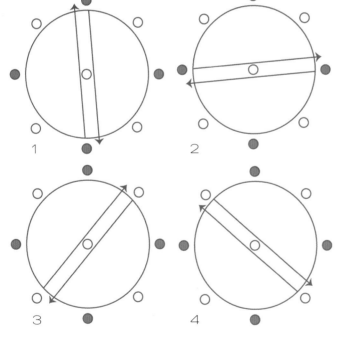

1

2

3

4

1 ➤ 16 then 17 ➤ 32
9 ➤ 24 then 25 ➤ 8
5 ➤ 19 then 21 ➤ 4
29 ➤ 12 then 13 ➤ 28

Point of braiding

After making the four pairs of moves the cords are still in straight lines in an eight-point star shape, but they've moved around anticlockwise to the next pair of slots to the left.

Round braid 2 variation

Starting position

To create bold stripes down the length of the braid, arrange your two colours of cord around the disk so that there are two adjacent cords in one colour then two in the alternate colour.

Round braid 2 textured

Although Kumihimo braids are generally worked with a smooth thread or cord most of the braids, including round braid 2, look very effective when braided with different thicknesses and textures of cord.

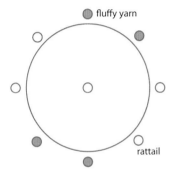

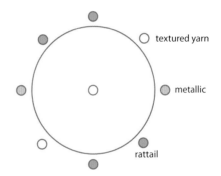

Variation 1

Add a fluffy textured yarn with smooth satin rattail to create an interesting contrast to the stripe variation for round braid 2.

Variation 2

The basic arrangement of alternate colours works well when alternating contrasting textures too. You can introduce a soft ribbon like organza or a silky mesh that will puff out, or add a metallic yarn for a bit of sparkle.

Starting position

fluffy yarn

rattail

Starting position

textured yarn

metallic

rattail

These delightful earrings are made from a fine Superlon™ cord for a firm braid that holds its shape well. Insert the raw ends into a decorative end cap and embellish with beads. For step-by-step instructions for making the Round Braid Earrings, see Projects.

Honeycomb braid

This variation of round braid 2 produces an unusual braid with long strands for a honeycomb effect.

Quick Guide: Honeycomb braid

Honeycomb braid is one of the most elegant braids and perhaps easier to work on a Marudai than on a disk because of the need to reposition the cords often; however, you can learn to swap the cords without needing to reposition (see Working from the Quick Guides: Repositioning Threads), which speeds up the braiding process. It is a variation of round braid 2, where the first two pairs of moves (vertical and horizontal) are repeated before completing the sequence with the diagonal moves. Use a thicker or stiffer cord for the vertical and horizontal cords to support and enhance any decorative strands in the diagonal slots.

Starting position

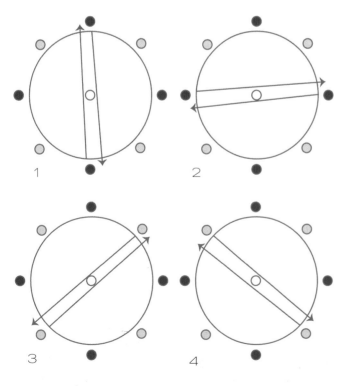

Remember, it is the diagonal cords that create the longer decorative strands on this braid.

Working the moves

Repeat the moves on diagrams 1 and 2 twice and reposition cords to the starting position, then work the moves on diagrams 3 and 4 and reposition again.

1 ➤ 16 then 17 ➤ 32

9 ➤ 24 then 25 ➤ 8

32 ➤ 15 then 16 ➤ 1

8 ➤ 23 then 24 ➤ 9

Reposition the straight cords: 15 to 17, 23 to 25.

5 ➤ 22 then 21 ➤ 5

29 ➤ 12 then 13 ➤ 29

Reposition the diagonal cords: 12 to 13, 22 to 21 ready to start again.

Point of braiding

To remind yourself how the sequence goes remember that the first four pairs of moves are straight, and the next two pairs of moves on the diagonal.

Honeycomb braid fancy cord variations

The honeycomb braid is ideal for showing the effects that can be achieved by experimenting with textural alternatives, as the following two examples show. The long strands look stunning when worked in a flat cord or ribbon. For other alternative cords, ribbons and threads that can be used in honeycomb braid see Cords and Threads for Kumihimo.

Variation 1

In this example stranded metallic embroidery thread is in the diagonal position and 7mm (⅜in) silk ribbon in the other slots, producing a lovely soft sparkly braid.

Starting position

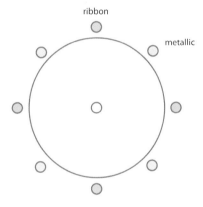

Variation 2

Silky mesh ribbon works well in the diagonal positions of honeycomb braid as the ribbon bunches out slightly adding extra texture. Rattail is used in the other slots.

Starting position

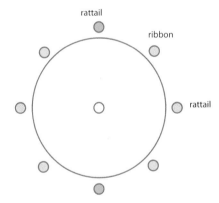

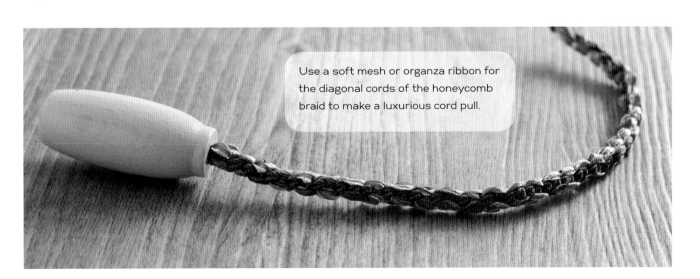

Use a soft mesh or organza ribbon for the diagonal cords of the honeycomb braid to make a luxurious cord pull.

103

Square braid

Even though this eight-strand braid has a square cross-section it is worked on a round disk or Marudai.

Quick Guide: Square braid

To preserve the square cross-section of this braid work with threads or cords all of the same thickness. The moves are simple – repeat the mantra: slide round then cross over. To make a sample braid, cut two 1m (1yd) lengths of 2mm rattail in two different colours and set up as shown, alternating the colours around the disk.

Starting position

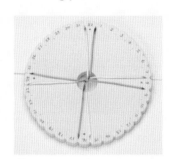

Basic Moves 3 and 6 are used and as both go around the edge of the disk, essentially the braid is hollow although it looks solid.

Working the moves

To remind yourself how the sequence goes, remember that the first two pairs of moves are clockwise and the next two anticlockwise.

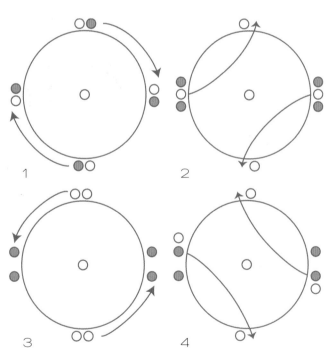

1 ➤ 7 then 17 ➤ 23

24 ➤ 1 then 8 ➤ 17

32 ➤ 26 then 16 ➤ 10

9 ➤ 32 then 25 ➤ 16

Reposition the side cords back to the starting slots (see the starting position photograph): 7 to 8 , 10 to 9, 26 to 25 and 23 to 24.

Point of braiding

After working the four pairs of moves, the top and bottom cords will be crossed over. You always move the underneath cord next.

Square braid variation

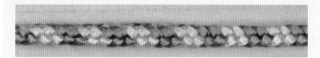

Starting position

Create a bolder V-shape pattern by changing the position of the colours. Start all four strands in the top half of the disk in one colour and another colour of cords in the bottom half.

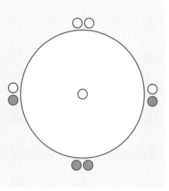

Square braid is a simple technique that works well in stiffer cords such as leather thong to create the framework for a stunning necklace. For step-by-step instructions for making the Square Braid Necklace, see Projects.

16-strand round braids

Once you have learnt to make an eight-strand round braid, add more strands to make a variety of 16-strand braids.

Quick Guide: 16-strand round braid four-colour spiral

Set up cords in the starting position then work the sequence as shown in the diagrams. The technique used is Basic Move 1 (see Basic Moves) and this is repeated although only the first four pairs of moves are shown. After that it is better to ignore the numbers and just repeat the moves as follows: top right cord to bottom right, bottom left cord to top left, then rotate one-eighth turn to the left.

To make a sample braid, cut four 1m (1yd) lengths of cotton perlé in four different colours and set up as shown with pairs of the same colour threads opposite each other around the disk.

Starting position

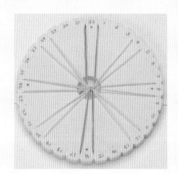

After each pair of moves rotate the disk one-eighth turn to the left so that the next colour is at the top and bottom.

Working the moves

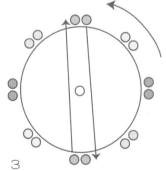

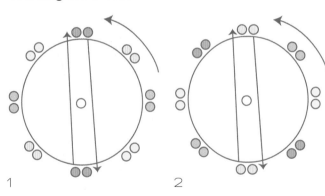

1

2

When learning to braid with 16 strands use four colours so that you can follow the pattern more easily. For this example I have used two strands of size 5 DMC cotton perlé for each bundle: pale peach (948), moss green (3052), pale yellow (745) and airforce blue (598).

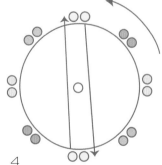

3

4

1 ➤ 15 then 17 ➤ 31

5 ➤ 19 then 21 ➤ 3

9 ➤ 23 then 25 ➤ 7

13 ➤ 27 then 29 ➤ 11

Point of braiding

After making four pairs of moves the colours have moved half way round; after eight pairs of moves the cords will be back in the start position.

16-strand round braid variations

Using these colour schemes as a guide, swap the colours matching the intensity of the hues to get a similar result or alter the colour balance and see what happens. By simply arranging colours in particular positions on the disk you can produce different patterns. Each of the following braids has a different arrangement using two strands each of two or three colours of size 5 DMC cotton perlé threads from the colour palette used to make the four-colour spiral, but you could experiment with four or more colours. The diagrams show the starting position for each pattern. Once you have set up, the technique is exactly the same as for the four-colour spiral: top right cord to bottom right, bottom left cord to top left, then rotate one-eighth turn to the left.

> With Kumihimo you can create a variety of differently patterned braids from the same technique simply by changing the positions and number of colours used.

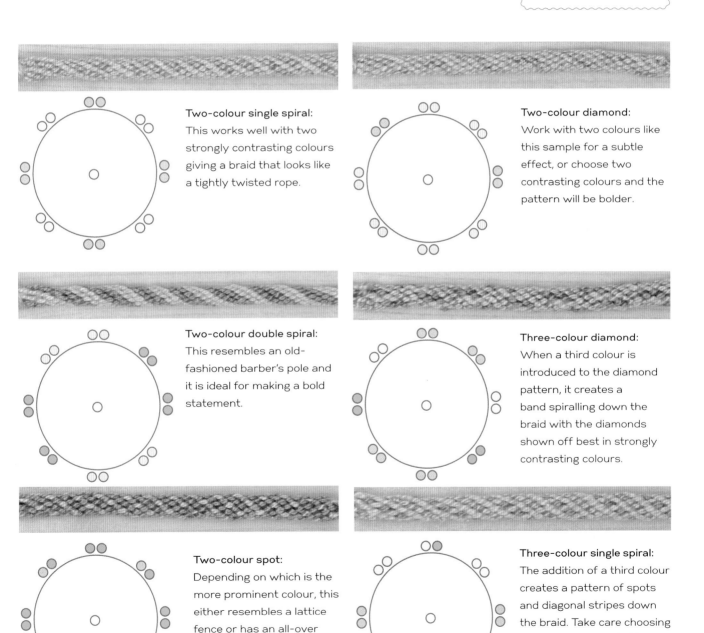

Two-colour single spiral:
This works well with two strongly contrasting colours giving a braid that looks like a tightly twisted rope.

Two-colour diamond:
Work with two colours like this sample for a subtle effect, or choose two contrasting colours and the pattern will be bolder.

Two-colour double spiral:
This resembles an old-fashioned barber's pole and it is ideal for making a bold statement.

Three-colour diamond:
When a third colour is introduced to the diamond pattern, it creates a band spiralling down the braid with the diamonds shown off best in strongly contrasting colours.

Two-colour spot:
Depending on which is the more prominent colour, this either resembles a lattice fence or has an all-over speckled appearance.

Three-colour single spiral:
The addition of a third colour creates a pattern of spots and diagonal stripes down the braid. Take care choosing the colours to create the best effect.

Helix Spiral Braids

These two spiral braids, worked with Basic Move 1 (see Basic Moves), are more textured than the standard eight-strand round braid spiral variations. They are double helix spirals, and this means that there are two different textures twisting around the braid like a corkscrew. The textures are created with short and long strands, and it is these longer strands that give the braids a silky luxurious look.

Helix spiral 1

Similar to round braid 1, this braid has three spiralling helixes, two with short strands and one with longer strands.

Quick Guide: Helix spiral 1

This attractive cord works well with satin cords in the side positions to create long lustrous strands. To make a sample braid, cut one 1m (1yd) length of rattail in tan and ivory and two lengths in dark brown, and set up as shown making sure that the ivory and tan colours are diagonally opposite each other. The colour scheme for Helix Spiral 1: has been chosen specifically so that you can see what positions on the disk create which helix, as an aid for designing your own colour schemes or changing textures of cord.

Starting position

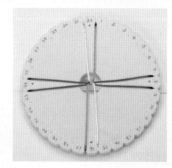

When setting up the disk, remember that the side cords create the longer strand helix and the top and bottom cords the shorter strand helix.

Working the moves

When working this braid some of the cords move out of position and after each sequence of three pairs of moves need to be placed back in the start position.

Point of braiding

Always move the top cord first and then, when you move the bottom cord up, you can put it in the vacated slot to avoid having to reposition the top cords.

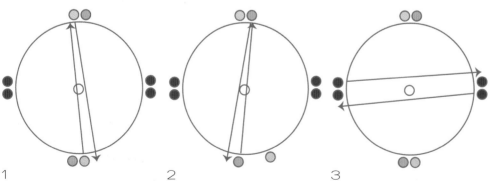

1   2   3

32 ➤ 15 then 16 ➤ 32

1 ➤ 18 then 17 ➤ 1

25 ➤ 7 then 9 ➤ 23

Reposition the bottom and side cords to the starting position after three pairs of moves: 8 to 9, 7 to 8, 15 to 16, 18 to 17, 24 to 25 and 23 to 24.

Helix spiral 2

This colour scheme chosen enables you to see the cord positions that create this attractive spiral braid.

Quick Guide: Helix spiral 2

This is a trickier spiral braid to make than helix spiral 1, as you need to support and adjust the cords as you braid. I hold the braid under the disk and twist after each move to align the cords neatly as shown in the point of braiding.

To make a sample braid, cut 1m (1yd) lengths of rattail in tan, ivory, lilac and dark brown. Set up as shown making sure that the ivory and tan colours are diagonally opposite. By positioning the side colours (top and bottom) diagonally opposite each other rather than straight across, the colours alternate along the braid.

Starting position

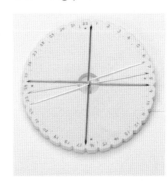

Choose your colour scheme carefully remembering that the side cords create the longer helix and the top and bottom cords the shorter helix.

Working the moves

The cords in this braid move around the disk and so after the first four pairs of moves you should refer to the diagrams but ignore the numbers. Although there are four pairs of moves, diagrams 1 and 2 are repeated.

Point of braiding

After four pairs of moves pinch the cords together where they cross so that it looks exactly as shown.

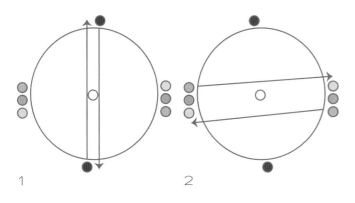

1

2

1 ➤ 16 then 17 ➤ 32
25 ➤ 6 then 9 ➤ 22
32 ➤ 15 then 16 ➤ 31
24 ➤ 5 then 8 ➤ 21

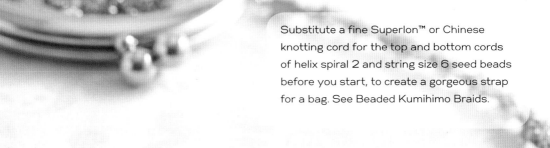

Substitute a fine Superlon™ or Chinese knotting cord for the top and bottom cords of helix spiral 2 and string size 6 seed beads before you start, to create a gorgeous strap for a bag. See Beaded Kumihimo Braids.

Hollow Braids

When working Kumihimo, if none of the moves go over the middle of the disk or Marudai, a braid is made that has a space down its centre. Depending on the number and thickness of the cords being worked with, the centre space can be narrow (see Square Braid) or large enough to insert a core cord – or even plastic tubing – into. Cord inserts in hollow braid make it much stronger, opening up the possibilities for its use. Several variations for hollow braids are described here, as well as instructions for inserting a core cord.

Adding a cord insert

Hollow braids can be worked with or without a core. The core fills the area inside the braid, and the basic principle is explained for the nine-strand hollow braid using a 550 paracord for the core cord.

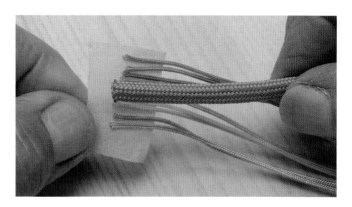

1 Arrange the braiding cords in the order that they will be on the disk following the starting position diagram/photograph, spacing them onto a piece of tape so that they will fit around the core cord. Wrap the tape around the base of the core cord.

2 Use a piece of strong thread to secure the cords above the tape, and tuck the cord bundle into the disk hole. Arrange the cords in the correct starting position for the braid and attach a weight to the end of the cords (see Preparing to Braid).

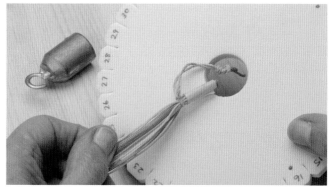

3 Work the braiding moves around the core cord, moving the core cord from side to side if necessary so that it is out of the way as you braid.

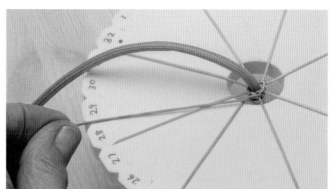

> Depending on the material used for the core cord, it can be very firm and suitable for using as either a light pull or bag handle or as a cord in contemporary jewellery.

Eight-strand hollow braid

This braid uses Basic Move 4, where a cord crosses over one stationary cord on each move.

Quick Guide: Eight-strand hollow braid

This sequence of moves takes a little getting used to, but it is an easy rhythmic braid once you get started. The moves go: top left to top right side, bottom right to bottom left side, then middle right to bottom right, middle left to top left, then top right to top left, bottom left to bottom right, and finally middle right to top right, middle left to bottom left.

The braid can be flattened or worked around a core cord to keep its round shape (see Adding a Cord Insert).

Starting position

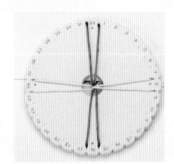

> To make a sample braid, cut two 1m (1yd) lengths of rattail in two contrasting colours and set up as shown with pairs of colours opposite each other.

Working the moves

When working on a disk, two of the side cords need to be repositioned back to the starting position every four pairs of moves.

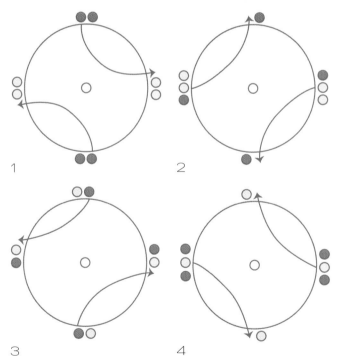

1

2

3

4

32 ➤ 7 then 16 ➤ 23

24 ➤ 32 then 8 ➤ 16

1 ➤ 26 then 17 ➤ 10

9 ➤ 1 then 25 ➤ 17

Reposition the side cords after four pairs of moves: 7 to 8, 10 to 9, 23; and after eight moves: 24, 26 to 25.

Point of braiding

After making four pairs of moves the position of the colours has swapped as shown here, but after eight pairs of moves they're back to the starting position.

Eight-strand hollow braid variation

Starting position

Although worked in exactly the same way as the main version of eight-strand hollow braid, this alternative produces an attractive spot pattern simply by changing the number of cords used of each colour. You'll need one 1m (1yd) length of grey and three 1m (1yd) lengths of green, set up as shown to make a sample.

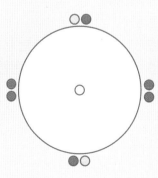

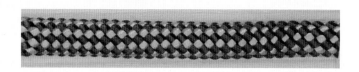

16-strand hollow braid

The 16-strand hollow braids are tubular but will flatten unless worked around a core plastic tubing for example for support.

Quick Guide: 16-strand hollow braid

This hollow braid uses Basic Move 2, where cords pass around the edge crossing over one stationary cord each time. The cords move clockwise for the first four pairs of moves, then anticlockwise for the second four pairs of moves. This adaptation of the traditional moves is easier to work on a disk where you use only one hand to move the cords.

To make a sample braid, cut four 1m (1yd) lengths of 1mm rattail in two different colours and set up with the colours alternating around the disk.

Starting position

This colour scheme makes it easy to learn the technique as the apricot cords all move clockwise then the plum cords all move anticlockwise.

Working the moves

On a disk you need to reposition the cords back into pairs side-by-side after four pairs of moves. Just remember, if you reposition clockwise then the next moves are anticlockwise, and vice versa.

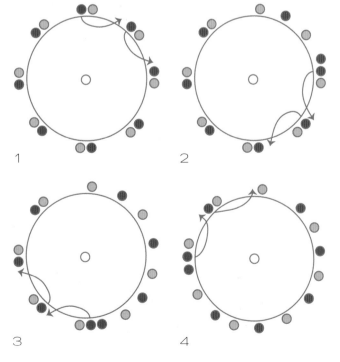

32 ➤ 3 then 4 ➤ 7

8 ➤ 11 then 12 ➤ 15

16 ➤ 19 then 20 ➤ 23,

24 ➤ 27 then 28 ➤ 31

Reposition clockwise: 3 to 4, 7 to 8, 11 to 12, 15 to 16, 19 to 20, 23 to 24 and 26 to 28.

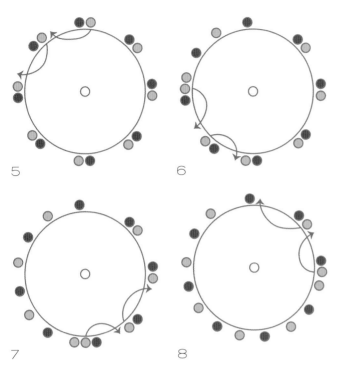

5

6

1 ➤ 30 then 29 ➤ 26

25 ➤ 22 then 21 ➤ 18

17 ➤ 14 then 13 ➤ 10

9 ➤ 6 then 5 ➤ 1

Reposition anticlockwise: 30 to 29, 26 to 25, 22 to 21, 18 to 17, 14 to 13, 10 to 9 and 6 to 5.

7

8

Point of braiding

Although this braid has been worked around a core, the point of braiding has been shown without the core for clarity.

Choose any of the 16-strand hollow braid patterns, such as the two-colour spiral shown here, and work a 16-strand hollow braid around a 6mm (¼in) diameter plastic tube, then remove the tube (see Removing the Core) and finish with end caps to make a very pretty bracelet. These end caps are designed for use with flat leather, but they hide the rattail raw ends very neatly (see Finishing Techniques for Braiding).

Removing the core

You can leave the core in place, but if you have used a smooth core, such as a piece of plastic tubing, it can be removed once you are finished, and then the braid can be flattened.

16-strand hollow braid variations

The 16-strand hollow braid technique gives you the chance to be creative with your colour choices, to make a variety of different patterns. As an example, a few samples have been worked using just three colours. Discover for yourself how, by selecting colours and arranging them in different slots, you can produce some precise patterns. Experiment with more than three colours to make your own unique designs.

Quick Guides: 16-strand hollow braid colour variations

These samples have been worked with various combinations of 1mm rattail in plum, apricot, teal, grey blue and gold, using no more than three colours for each. All the samples have been worked around 6mm (¼in) plastic tubing.

Work the hollow braids around a 6mm rope for a supple braid or around a plastic tube to make a bracelet.

Two-colour spiral

Using only two colours and arranging them in pairs around the disk creates a bold spiral pattern.

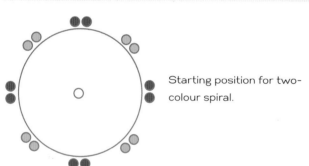

Starting position for two-colour spiral.

Three-colour speckle spiral

Careful colour positioning creates one strong spiral with a speckled spiral in between.

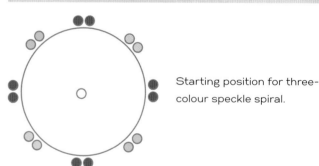

Starting position for three-colour speckle spiral.

Three-colour speckle

Tiny flecks of bright coral and teal on a grey background creates a pretty all-over pattern.

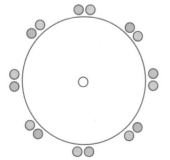

Starting position for three-colour speckle.

Four-colour spiral

Using a thicker rattail (2mm rather than 1mm) for the plum spiral raises the apricot and creates a rib effect.

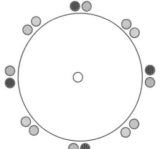

Starting position for four-colour spiral

Nine-strand hollow braid

This quick and easy hollow braid just uses Basic Move 5 repeated around and around the disk.

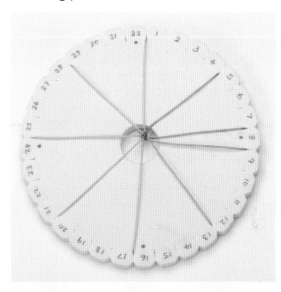

Quick Guide: Nine-strand hollow braid

Set up the cords as in the starting position. An extra cord (starting top side right) moves around the outer edge, crossing over two stationary cords at a time. If you want to add a core as shown in the finished sample photograph, see Adding a Cord Insert. Choose a strong contrast colour for the extra cord to emphasize the spiral effect. To make a sample braid, cut two 50cm (½yd) lengths of size 8 Chinese knotting cord in four different colours (olive, lime, grey and dark grey were used) plus an extra length of cord in dark grey. Tie in an overhand knot and set up the disk as shown (see Preparing to Braid).

You could make the braid with more cords so long as the main cords are spaced equally around the core with an extra cord placed in the slot above the right side cord ready to start.

Starting position

Working the moves

As you move the extra cord lift it up so that it is vertical and tug gently to position the cord correctly each time for a neat point of braiding in the centre.

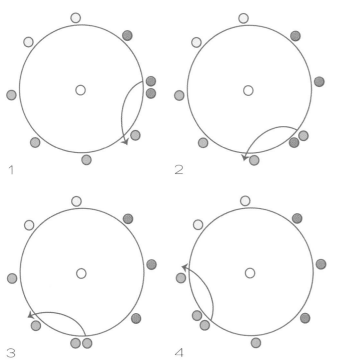

1

2

3

4

8 ➤ 14 then 13 ➤ 18

17 ➤ 22 then 21 ➤ 26

25 ➤ 30 then 29 ➤ 2

1 ➤ 6 then 5 ➤ 10

9 ➤ 15 then 14 ➤ 19

18 ➤ 23 then 22 ➤ 27

26 ➤ 31 then 30 ➤ 3

2 ➤ 7 then 6 ➤ 11 and so on.

Point of braiding

You can stop at any point on this sequence, as you are always ready to move the extra cord over the next two cords.

Flat Braids

Flat braids are worked on a square plate with a rectangular hole – the straight edge of the hole makes it easier to keep the braid flat. A step-by-step photo guide is provided for making a rounded flat braid so that you can familiarize yourself with the moves for using a square plate. These guides show how to create different flat braids: some straight, some woven on the diagonal, and some varying in width depending on the number of cords.

Using a square plate to make a rounded flat braid

This braid with a slightly domed top surface is an easy, rhythmic braid to work – ideal for a first attempt on the Kumihimo square plate.

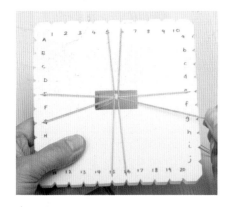

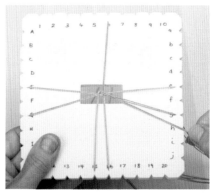

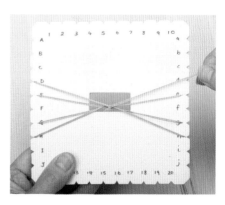

1 Choose two colours of cord and set up the plate as shown in the Quick Guide: Rounded Flat Braid. Attach a loop and weight (see Preparing to Braid). Here I have used two strands of size 5 nylon knotting cord for each bundle.

2 As you move the cords, hold the plate in one corner in the same hand all the time. Move the top left cord to the slot under the cords on the right side (from 5 to h as shown), then move the top right cord to the slot under the cords on the left side (from 6 to H).

3 Move the bottom right cord to the slot above the cords on the left side (from 16 to D), then move the bottom left cord to the slot above the cords on the right side (from 15 to d as shown).

> When you want to take a break from braiding, work to the end of the sequence and reposition the cords so that you are ready to start again.

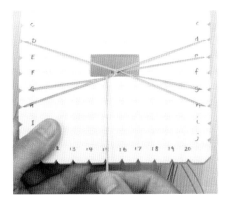 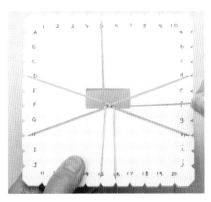 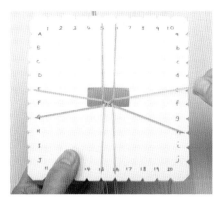

4 Move the second from top cords on both sides one at a time down to the centre slots at the bottom of the plate without crossing them over (E to 15 as shown, then e to 16).

5 Move the middle cords on both sides one at a time up to the centre slots at the top of the plate (from G to 5, then g to 6 as shown) to complete the four-pair move sequence.

6 Reposition the side cords back to the starting position by moving the top side cords down a slot and the bottom side cords up a slot, working one side at a time (from D to E and H to G, then d to e and h to g).

Worked in rounded flat braid technique, these pretty braids make quick and easy bracelets. Make them in co-ordinating colours and add beads to some for added texture and sparkle as shown in Beaded Kumihimo Braids. For step-by-step instructions for making the Stacking Beaded Bracelets, see Projects.

Quick Guide: Rounded flat braid

Set up cords in the starting position, then work the sequence as shown in the diagrams. Although illustrated in a square diagram this braid uses Basic Move 6 (see Basic Moves) where the cords being moved cross over each other and two other stationary cords. The pattern is determined by the way the colours are arranged on the plate: in the sample shown the vertical colour at the top of the plate will be the colour on the outer edges of the finished braid, and the one at the bottom is the colour of the centre stripe.

Starting position

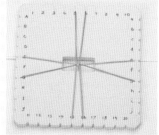

Working the moves

After making four pairs of moves reposition the side cords ready to begin again.

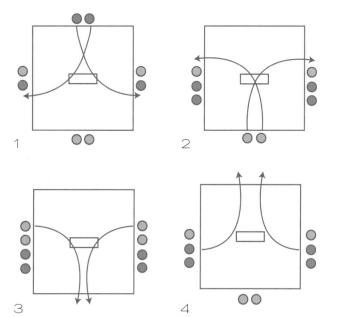

1

2

3

4

5 ➤ h then 6 ➤ H

16 ➤ D then 15 ➤ d

E ➤ 15 then e ➤ 16

G ➤ 5 then g ➤ 6

Reposition the side cords: D to E, H to G then d to e, h to g.

Point of braiding

When working flat braids, keep the braid flat against the edge of the rectangular hole for a better tension

Rounded flat braid variation

For a different effect with zigzag stripes try the colours arranged in the alternative starting position shown. This variation also looks quite different on its reverse side (see bottom sample)

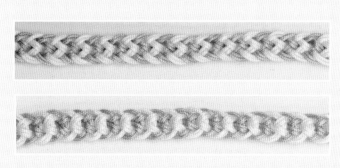

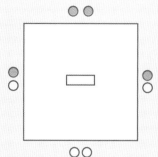

Starting position

This arrangement of colours, with one colour in the top half of the plate and the second colour in the bottom half, makes an attractive zigzag pattern.

Eight-strand flat braid

This flat braid is worked with eight strands of cord on a square plate and looks the same on both sides.

Quick Guide: Eight-strand flat braid with diagonal stripe

Set up cords in the starting position, then work the sequence as shown in the diagrams. Place one colour in the top and bottom positions and the other colour into the side slots to create the stripe. When working this braid it is essential to reposition the side cords to the starting position at the end of every four-pair sequence.

Starting position

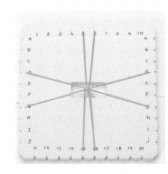

With this starting position you create a braid with a strong diagonal pattern that could look interesting worked in different textures of cords.

Working the moves

This braid uses Basic Move 5 where each cord is moved around the edge across two stationary cords. After making four pairs of moves reposition the side cords ready to begin again.

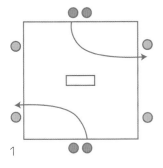
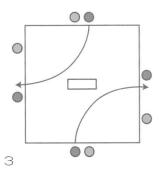

1

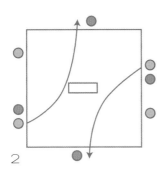
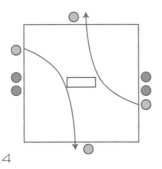

3

2

4

Point of braiding

When working this braid it helps to pinch the vertical cords together after you have repositioned the side cords ready to start the sequence again.

Eight-strand flat braid with zigzag variation

By arranging the colours in this alternative starting position, fine zigzag stripes going along the length of the braid can be achieved.

5 ➤ e then 16 ➤ F

d ➤ 16 then G ➤ 5

6 ➤ E then 15 ➤ f

g ➤ 6 then D ➤ 15

Reposition the side cords: E to D, e to d and F to G, f to g.

Starting position

This colour pattern is achieved by keeping all the cords on the left of the centre line in one colour and those on the right a contrast colour.

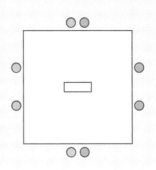

Woven Flat Braids

Woven flat braids look quite different to the other flat braids. Traditionally known as Anda-gumi, these braids have a similar structure to a plain, woven fabric where the weft threads go alternately over and under the warp threads. The same technique used to make the Anda-gumi can create a zigzag braid, and for both it is better to work without a weight, holding the braid flat against the edge of the plate's rectangular slot.

Using a square plate to make a woven flat braid

Set up cords in the starting position then work the sequence as shown in the diagrams. and follow the step-by-step photo guide.

Starting position

1 Choose three colours of cord and set up the plate as shown. This arrangement of colours gives a fairly random pattern on the braid but you can experiment with two or more colours to create a wide range of designs. For this example I have used two strands of size 5 cotton perlé for each bundle. Attach a loop (see Preparing to Braid) then add a weight.

> The moves for woven flat braid are quite different to regular Kumihimo. Take care to work through each stage from setting up to working the braid and it will soon seem quite simple.

Start move

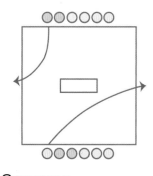

START MOVE

13 ➤ E then 3 ➤ e

2 To work the start sequence: take the bottom left cord and move it to a left side slot (13 to E as shown) and then take the top left cord and move it to a right side slot (3 to e). These become the weft threads. This pair of moves is not repeated.

Move 1: Bottom and top cords change places

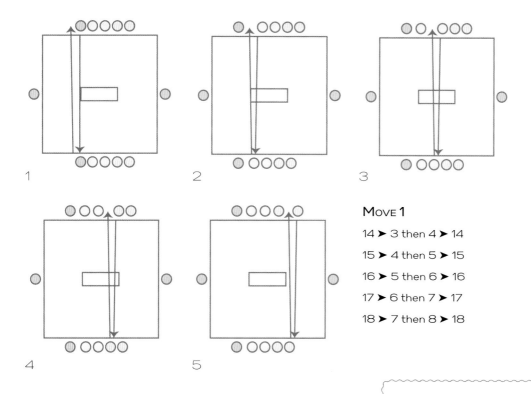

1

2

3

4

5

MOVE 1

14 ➤ 3 then 4 ➤ 14

15 ➤ 4 then 5 ➤ 15

16 ➤ 5 then 6 ➤ 16

17 ➤ 6 then 7 ➤ 17

18 ➤ 7 then 8 ➤ 18

Once you have completed the start sequence,
the braid is 'woven' by repeating Moves 1 and 2..

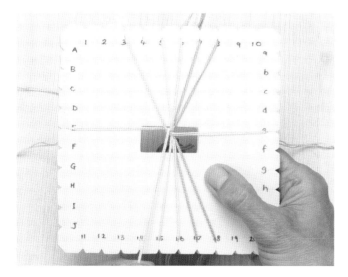

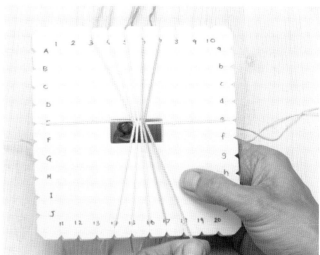

3 To 'weave' the warp: take the bottom left cord and move it to the empty slot left of the cords on the top edge (14 to 3 as shown), and then take the next top left cord and move it to the empty slot left of the cords on the bottom edge (4 to 14).

4 To move the rest of the warp threads, working from the left, take the next bottom cord and move it to the empty slot on the top edge. Take the next top cord and move it to the empty slot on the bottom edge. Repeat to swap all the cords from the bottom to the top and vice versa.

Move 2: Setting up the new weft cords

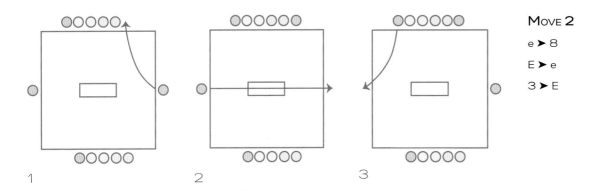

1   2   3

MOVE 2

e ➤ 8

E ➤ e

3 ➤ E

5 To create the next weft: take the right side cord and move it to the top right slot (e to 8 as shown). Then take the left side cord and move it the middle slot on the right side (E to e as shown). Finally take the top left cord and move it to the middle slot on the left side. (3 to E).

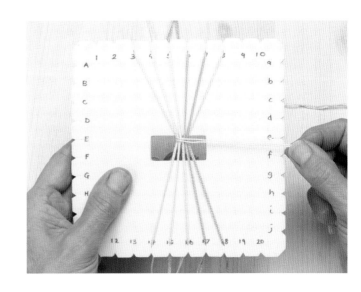

Point of braiding

As with all flat braids, you get a more even result if you hold the braid flat against the side of the slot as you work

Repeat Moves 1 and 2

6 Repeat steps 3–5 to work the braid. The sequence will be the same but the colours will move to the left each time.

Zigzag woven flat braid

One of the most attractive variations of the woven flat braid technique is the ric-rac braid, which is made by turning the plate upside down at regular intervals.

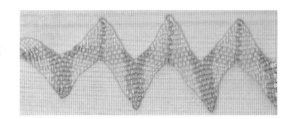

Working the moves for zigzag woven flat braid

This braid may seem daunting as there are more moves and diagrams than usual. This is because the plate is turned upside down every time you want to make the sharp zigzag and so, although some of the basic moves are the same as the straight version of the woven flat braid, others use the same diagram but the numbers are different because the plate is upside down. Where necessary you'll be referred back to Using a Square Plate to Make Woven Flat Braid. Moves 1a and 2a, for example, follow diagrams for Move 1 and 2.

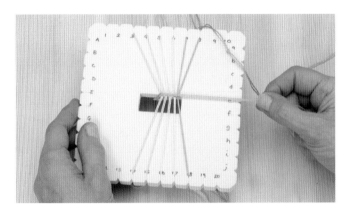

1 Work with three colours of cord and set up the plate (see Woven Flat Braid, step 1). Tie a knot in the top right cord. *Begin with the Start Move, then work Move 1 and Move 2 sequences (see Woven Flat Braid, steps 2–6) until the cord with the knot has been moved into slot e to become the new weft as shown.

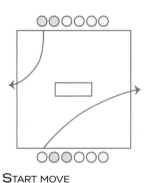

START MOVE

13 ➤ E then 3 ➤ e

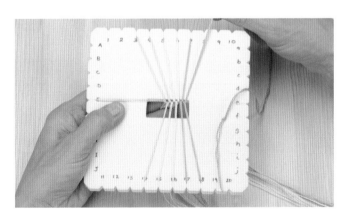

2 To set up the cords ready to rotate the plate, work the Move 1 sequence once more (see Woven Flat Braid, diagrams 1–5). Move the cord with the knot from the right side to the top right (e to 8) as shown, then move the left side cord to the bottom left (E to 13) following the Rotate 1 diagram.

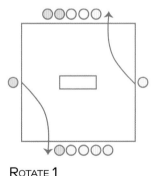

ROTATE 1

e ➤ 8 then E ➤ 13

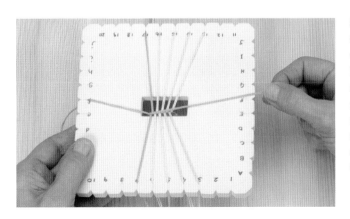

3 To start the zigzag, turn the plate upside down and work the Start 1 sequence. Move the top left to the left side (18 to f as shown), then move the bottom left to the right side (8 to F). Adjust the cords so that the braid is flat against the opposite side of the slot (new top edge).

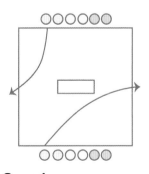

START 1

18 ➤ f

8 ➤ F

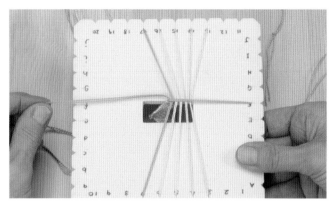

4 Work the Move 1a and 2a sequences until the marker thread is in the right side slot again (F). Work the Move 1a sequence once more.

Move 1a (see woven flat braid, move 1)

7 ➤ 18 then 17 ➤ 7

6 ➤ 17 then 16 ➤ 6

5 ➤ 16 then 15 ➤ 5

4 ➤ 15 then 14 ➤ 4

3 ➤ 14 then 13 ➤ 3

Move 2a (see woven flat braid, move 2)

F ➤ 13

f ➤ F

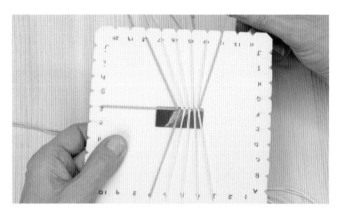

5 Then, following the Rotate 2 diagram, move the cord from the right side to the top right (F to 13 as shown), then move the left side cord to the bottom left (f to 8). Turn the disk the right way up.

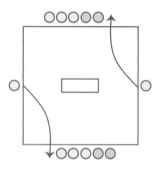

Rotate 2

F ➤ 13 then f ➤ 8

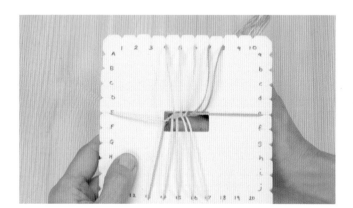

6 Repeat from * to create the zigzag braid, remembering to adjust the cords so that the braid is against the opposite side of the slot (top edge).

Every time you turn the plate you make a right angle to create a zigzag along the length. You can work longer or shorter distances between the rotate moves to vary the look of the braid.

Beaded Kumihimo Braids

Kumihimo braids can be easily embellished with beads for even more stunning effects, Beads can be threaded or stitched onto the finished braids, strung onto the cords before braiding, or added in as the braiding is worked. The samples I have made are designed to give you a flavour of what can be achieved. For more information on beads that can be used with Kumihimo see Essential Equipment.

Choosing beads

Beads come in a huge variety of shapes, sizes and colours, not to mention the wide range of different materials, so it should be easy to find a bead suitable for adding to your Kumihimo braids. Depending on the technique you choose, it is often the hole size that is more important rather than the bead itself, as the beads often have either to thread onto a cord or onto the braid itself.

Adding beads while braiding

Beads can be added to some or all of the cords before you start braiding. Be inspired by the examples shown, then learn the techniques, which can be used for all types of braid – flat, round, square or hollow.

Stringing seed beads

If you are using a stiff threading medium like Superlon™, seed beads (size 8 or 6) can be strung onto it easily without using a needle. Otherwise, use one of the following techniques to string the beads.

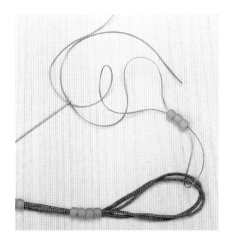

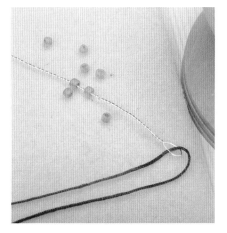

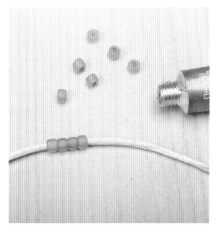

Fold a strong fine thread or wire in half and thread the tails into a needle. Feed a thicker strand through the loop of finer thread or wire. This allows you to thread small hole beads onto the needle and onto the thicker strand.

Use a twisted wire needle to pick beads up one at a time from a beading mat, or for large quantities use a bead spinner to add beads quickly to the strands before braiding.

Apply a little glue or nail varnish to the end of strands or thicker cord, then smooth between finger and thumb to create a 'needle' once dry.

Step-by-step guide to braiding with beads

The basic technique for adding beads as you braid is similar regardless of the type of Kumihimo braid being worked; for the purposes of the step sequence, the technique is being shown applied to an eight-strand round braid.

To make a sample braid, cut two 1m (1yd) lengths of 2mm rattail, one in plum and one in peach, and two 1m (1yd) lengths of Superlon™, one in dark grey and one in peach. String size 8 (3mm) Toho seed beads on the cords as follows: matte tea rose 155F and dark peach lined 275 on peach Superlon™; ceylon grey 150 and dark peach-lined 275 on grey Superlon™.

Starting position

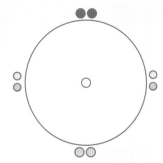

Set up cords in the starting position then work the sequence as shown in the diagrams for Eight-strand Round Braid.

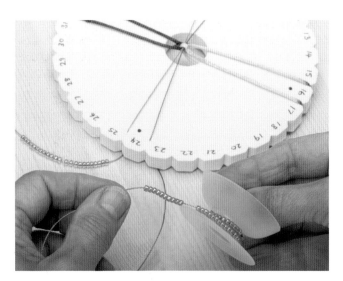

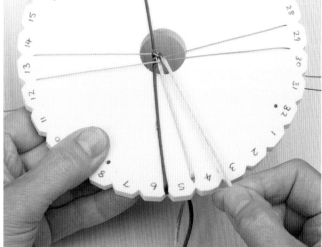

1 Set up the disk as shown in the starting position diagram. Thread beads onto the four thin Superlon™ strands: dark peach and matte rose on the peach Superlon™, grey and dark peach on the grey Superlon™. You will need about 22 beads for every 5cm (2in) length of beaded cord. If the cords are over 50cm (½yd) in length, wind them onto bobbins.

2 On shorter strands for a bracelet, you don't need to use a bobbin – simply tie a knot at the end. Attach a weight to the loop in the middle of the strands. Work at least 1cm (³⁄₈in) of the basic round braid (see Eight-strand Round Braid) without beads, more if you want plain cord at each end of the braid.

To create your own colour scheme for the basic beaded round braid think of the colours as dark and light.

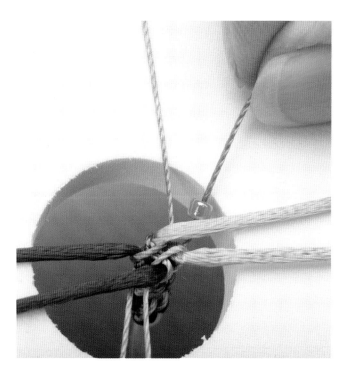

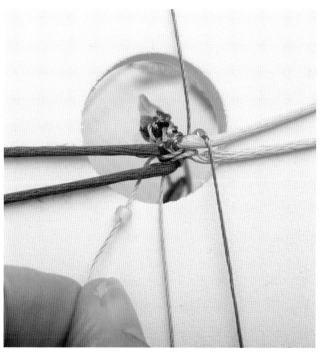

3 Lift the top right Superlon™ strand and let a bead drop down to the point of braiding. Push the bead under the top horizontal rattail strand and then place the Superlon™ in the bottom right slot.

4 Lift the bottom left Superlon™ strand and let a bead drop down to the point of braiding again. This time tuck the bead under the bottom horizontal rattail strand, then place the Superlon™ in the top left slot.

5 Rotate the disk a quarter turn to the left and move the rattail strands in order, making sure that the beads stay tucked away below the point of braiding.

6 Continue adding one bead at a time when you move the thinner Superlon™ strands, making sure you do so or there will be gaps in the beading. Finish the braid by working at least 1cm (³/₈in) without beads.

Some beaded braid samples

Beads can be added to any of the braids in this book, either on all of the strands or on just some of the strands. When adding seed beads, you will need to incorporate a thinner thread or cord so that these can be threaded on (see Stringing Seed Beads).

Eight-strand round braid sampler

This long sample shows how a variety of different beads look when incorporated into the same basic braid to illustrate the huge potential for designing braids with beads. It is worked with a stiff nylon cord (Superlon™), which although fine, has enough body to support the beads.

Details of beads used:

(1) 3mm square and 4mm round fire-polished beads

(2) 3mm glass pearl beads

(3) 7 x 4mm long Magatamas

(4) 2mm bicone crystals and size 15 delicas

(5) Size 8 and size 11 seed beads

(6) Size 8 seed beads

(7) Farfalle or peanut beads

(8) 4mm bicone crystals

(9) Double delicas

(10) Size 6 seed beads

Helix spiral 1

Using different weights of cord causes the braid to flatten rather than twist. Rattail is used in the top and bottom positions. Add beads to the peach and grey Superlon™ diagonally opposite at the sides.

Honeycomb braid

Set up the disk for this braid with rattail for the horizontal and vertical cords and Superlon™ for the diagonal cords, stringing a mix of size 8 seed beads and size 11 triangle beads. Incorporate three beads into the braid each time you move a diagonal cord.

Adding beads after braiding

The easiest way to add beads is simply to string beads onto the finished braid, but beads can also be sewn on too.

Preparing the ends

Kumihimo braids are created under tension so that they are tightly woven, and the end will unravel when the cords are cut making it difficult to string on beads. If you started your braid with a lark's head knot (see Preparing to Braid), there will be a rounded end that will pass through a large hole bead, otherwise try one of the techniques shown below to prepare the ends of the braid for stringing.

Threading beads onto the braids

Beads can be strung directly onto the braids, but you may need to prepare the ends first. If the bead fits snugly over the cord it may stay in position as the braid expands slightly on either side, otherwise apply a little glue onto the braid before sliding the bead on top to secure.

* Divide the loose cords in half and pull one half through using a large tapestry needle, then pull the other half through.

* Whip the end of the cords with a fine sewing thread and sew in the ends. Apply a little glue to smooth any stray ends and leave to dry before stringing the beads.

* Alternatively feed a fine wire or strong thread through behind the whipping, then use as a needle to string the beads.

Ideas for stringing beads

* Lots of beads, like pony beads and Pandora-style beads, have large holes that can be strung onto Kumihimo braids. Take care to match the diameter of the braid to the hole size.

* Thinner braids can be used to string beads pendant-style. Use a small bead as a 'turn' bead below the larger bead or above the larger bead for a different look.

* Use large hole beads to create a figure of eight band, threading two braids in opposite directions through the beads.

Sewing beads into the braid

Beads can be stitched into the braids to add further embellishment. When placing the beads, work with the shape and pattern of the finished braid to enhance the cord design. Use shaped beads that will sit into the braid such as drops or magatamas, or add texture with triangle beads, hex beads or tiny seed beads.

1 Secure a strong beading thread into the braid using tiny backstitches. Feed the needle through the middle of the braid and bring it out where you want the bead to sit.

2 Pick up a seed bead and stitch back into the braid, going back through the bead one more time to attach it securely. Take the needle through the middle of the braid to come out where you want to stitch on the next bead.

3 When sewing beads on the edge of the braid, either sew through at a diagonal, or straight across as shown, to add a few beads at a time. When sewing groups of beads like this, stitch with a double thread for extra strength.

Ideas for sewing in beads

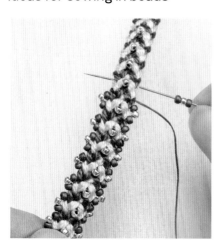

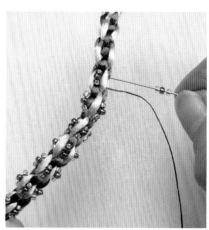

★ Stitch beads on individually so that they sit attractively in each chevron then embellish further with loops down each edge of the rounded flat braid.

★ Trap beads. by sewing between two strands of braiding such as the square braids used in this example.

★ Sew loops of beads between the longer strands on honeycomb braid to add extra texture and colour.

> Always anchor beading thread with two or three tiny backstitches rather than a knot that may come undone or pull through.

Working with Wire

Kumihimo is a versatile technique that can be worked in a range of different materials including wire, which has many exciting possibilities. You can use wire to make the entire braid or just introduce it on some strands, and you can work hollow braids around a wire core for flexible curves. Wire can also be added to a finished braid as a decorative embellishment.

Choosing wire

So long as the wire is soft enough to be manipulated and not so brittle that it breaks readily it can be used for Kumihimo – see Kumihimo: Equipment and Materials for more information. Wire is sold either by measurement or gauge: the thinner the wire, the larger the gauge and any wire between 0.2mm (36swg) and 0.6mm (24swg) would be suitable. Thicker wires are harder to bend but you can buy soft aluminium wires or silver wire in a soft condition for a special project.

* Several strands of a thin wire is easier to work than the equivalent thicker wire, for example use four strands of 0.315mm (30swg) wire rather than a 1.2mm (18swg) wire.
* When working with four or more wire strands it's necessary to really pull the wire into position at the point of braiding to make a more even braid.
* Fewer wires in each bundle will give a smoother braid: an eight-strand round braid with four wires in each bundle will be more textured than a 16-strand round braid with two wires in each bundle.

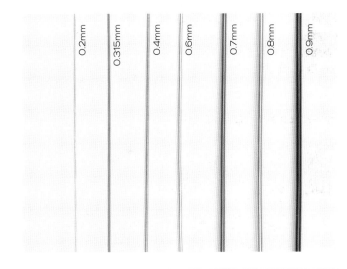

0.2mm   0.315mm   0.4mm   0.6mm   0.7mm   0.8mm   0.9mm

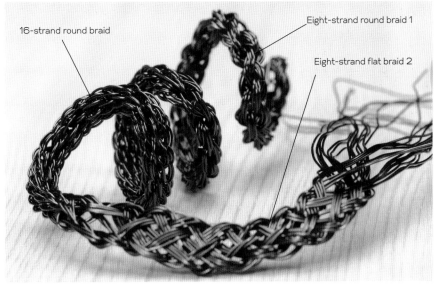

16-strand round braid

Eight-strand round braid 1

Eight-strand flat braid 2

Kumihimo braids worked in wire will hold their shape when curved or bent. This piece has three different braids worked on the one piece, and making a sample like this, changing from one technique to another that has the same set up, will give you a quick introduction to the possibilities when working with wire.

Because of its strong structure, wire can be used in Kumihimo to make pieces of jewellery like this fabulous brooch. It is made from a 16-strand hollow braid that is flattened and shaped before being embellished with beads. For step-by-step instructions for making the Kumihimo Hollow Braid Brooch, see Projects.

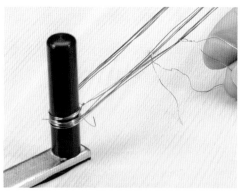

Getting started with wire

Unlike cords and threads, wire has no stretch so it cannot be worked at an even tension but must be carefully placed into position. Mistakes must be avoided as kinked wire will look unsightly when reworked.

Preparing the wire
For lengths of wire in excess of 50cm (20in)

1 Clamp two upright pegs to the work surface or use one peg in a vice and hold the other. Space the pegs the length you need for the braid (see Preparing to Braid). Secure the wire with a twisted loop at one end and begin to wind the wire around both pegs keeping a fairly good tension.

2 When working with thin wire you can use multiple strands for each bundle. Once you have wound sufficient strands for a bundle, tie a piece of thread or cord around the bundle. Don't cut the wire yet – keep winding until you have tied all the bundles.

3 Secure one end of the wires together with a twist of wire or cord before you remove them from the pegs. Snip through the wires one bundle at a time and wind the bundle of wires onto a bobbin ready to start the Kumihimo. Set up the disk as shown in Preparing to Braid.

For a bracelet length
Simply wind wire around a 45cm (18in) ruler. Hold the first colour at one end and count the number of lengths you need, say 8 or 16 wraps. Repeat with the second colour.

Wire has a tendency to spring back when released, so take care to hold the cut ends and release slowly to prevent any accidents.

Working flat braids with wire

These are a good place to start for a first try with wire as it is easier to move the wires into the correct position when working with a flat braid rather than a round one, and you don't need to worry about getting an even 3D shape. Although you would normally use a square plate, you can quite easily make these two sample braids on a round disk too.

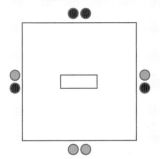

Depending on where you place the colours there are a variety of colour patterns that can be worked in rounded flat braid. See Rounded Flat Braid Variation for this pattern.

Quick Guide: Rounded flat braid in wire

With this set up there is a colour border and a chevron band down the centre as shown in the pendant below. Cut eight 90cm (36in) lengths of 0.4mm (27swg) wire in each of two different colours. Fold the wires in half and secure with a cord loop or twist of wire. Set up four wires into each slot with the colours arranged as shown in the starting position diagram, then work the sequence as shown for Rounded Flat Braid. Once you have worked the flat braid and removed it from the disk or plate, pull the ends firmly to even up the wirework.

Starting position

> Moving the wire into position can be quite hard on the hands, especially when trying to keep a good tension. I find several strands of a thinner wire are easier to work with than one or two thick wires.

Although it works very well as a straight band for a bracelet, the rounded flat braid can easily be shaped into a curve or circle to create an attractive pendant or ring component for jewellery designs. To make the ring pendant, trim the tails and overlap, then sew together with a piece of wire. Make a wrapped loop in the middle of a double length of wire, then wrap the tails around to hide the overlapping ends. Add a chain or leather cord to hang.

Quick Guide: Woven flat braid

Cut eight 90cm (36in) lengths of 0.4mm (27swg) wire in each of two different colours. Fold the wires in half and secure with a cord loop or twist of wire. Set up the wires as shown in the starting position diagram, then work the sequence as shown in the diagrams. Remember, once you have worked the braid and removed it from the disk or plate, pull the ends firmly to even up.

This braid can be made with cord but when worked in wire it works well as a flat band for a bracelet. Attach rectangular end caps and a fastening to finish (see Finishing Techniques for Braiding).

Working the moves

This braid was the result of a happy accident. I tried to remember the sequence for rounded flat braid off the top of my head and created this woven effect that works very well in wire.

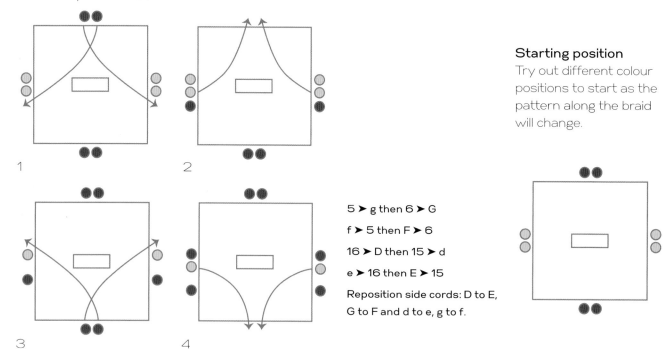

1

2

3

4

Starting position

Try out different colour positions to start as the pattern along the braid will change.

5 ➤ g then 6 ➤ G

f ➤ 5 then F ➤ 6

16 ➤ D then 15 ➤ d

e ➤ 16 then E ➤ 15

Reposition side cords: D to E, G to F and d to e, g to f.

Working round braids with wire

All the round braids, including helix spirals and hollow braids, can be worked in wire and it is worth trying out short sections of different braids to see what effects you get.

Try using two or more strands of a thin wire such as 0.315mm (30swg) or 0.4mm (27swg) so that it is fairly easy to work, or try adding beads to a single 0.6mm (24swg) wire or even a thicker soft aluminium wire.

Working with wire and cords

Mixing wire and cords in your Kumihimo braids is very effective as the softness of the thread combines with the hard edge of the wire.

Choosing where to put the wire

Every braid will have variations depending on which cord bundles are changed to wire. You can add one or two strands of thin wire to each bundle so that the braid can be manipulated into shape without changing the original look too much, but it is much more exciting to replace some of the strands with wire instead of cord.

As you experiment you'll find that the same braid can look quite different with the wire in different starting positions. Wires at the side starting positions will make a spiral braid, but put the wires in the top and bottom slots to start, and you will create a flatter braid with cord on the outside and wire down the centre. The wire prevents the braid twisting so it can be flat or you can twist it once complete.

S-shape spiral: Wire has been used in the top and bottom slots and cords in the side positions to create a neat spiral.

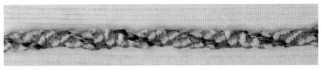

Place two or three fine wires in the horizontal position across the disk to start.

Round braid 2: There are four cords and four bundles of four wires alternating so that in the start position the wires are top to bottom and side to side and the cords are on the diagonals.

Start with four fine wires in the vertical position to create this strong spiral.

Adding wire into Kumihimo braid allows the braid to be bent or twisted to hold a particular shape. Try making one or two different thicknesses of round braids to create a pretty brooch or corsage, adding sparkly crystals on twisted wire stems to finish.

Finishing Techniques for Braiding

Kumihimo braids have many raw ends that need to be neatened in some way before they can be made into a piece of jewellery, accessory or other item. Traditional techniques such as whipping or wrapping can be used to cover the raw ends, or you can use specially designed findings such as end caps or cones (see Essential Equipment). It is also possible to add large and small beads for a more decorative embellishment.

Finishing flat Kumihimo braids

Rectangular end caps are ideal for finishing the ends of flat Kumihimo braids.
Use the internal measurement of the finding as a guide to getting the right fit.

1 Before you trim the braid, sew across near the end using a strong beading or sewing thread. Stitch running stitches in one direction and then sew back across. Sew in the thread ends with a couple of tiny backstitches.

2 Trim the braid close to the stitching, but not so close that the threads pull out. Trim the outer edges carefully to make it easier to insert the braid into the end cap.

3 Apply glue inside the end cap (not on the braid) with a cocktail stick. For a flat braid it is easier to get one end of the braid in and then to use an awl or large tapestry needle to work along the edge, then push in the remaining bit. Repeat to attach an end cap at the other end.

The stitch-and-trim method can also be used to neaten the end of Kumihimo braids or plaiting before attaching a ribbon crimp end. Nylon-jaw pliers will prevent the crimp end from being damaged as it is pressed to secure.

Finishing round Kumihimo braids

Depending on the braiding technique and the thread or cord used, round braids may fit in a cord end, or a large end cap or cone may be required. A selection of braids together with suitable findings are pictured here, and the techniques of adding end caps or cones and attaching a wire loop are explained in detail in Essential Techniques.

★ Thin braids worked with Superlon™ or other fine cords can be glued into a cord end. It will help to wrap even these tiny braids with sewing thread before inserting them into the finding.

★ When working with wire braids, simply twist the end of the wires, then trim the end neatly before gluing it into the end cap or cone.

★ Hollow braids with a core can be finished with an end cap. Wrap thread around the braid near the top of the core and then trim any braid sticking above the core before attaching the end cap.

Finishing plaited braids

Although plaiting is a simple technique, it can be worked with a variety of different cords and threads, so there are many different ways to neaten the ends. A selection of plaited braids together with suitable findings are pictured here. For how to fit end caps or cones, suitable for more rounded plaiting, see Finishing Techniques, and for suitable techniques for attaching a finding to a flat plaited braid see Finishing Flat Kumihimo Braids.

★ Ribbon crimps are suitable for finishing thin flat plaiting. They are available in several widths. Sew the strands together, then trim in a straight line before attaching the ribbon crimp with nylon-jaw pliers.

★ Wrap round plaited bundles with sewing thread before attaching an end cap with glue. You can insert a headpin under the wrapping to make a loop if required.

★ Large bundles of different materials plaited together can be finished with an end cone. Wrap the end of the bundle with wire and then attach the end cone with a little glue, adding a loop to finish.

Using beads to cover raw ends

Although end caps or cones are often used to finish the ends of Kumihimo braid, when a fastening is not required beads can be used to cover the raw ends or to hide a join.

Finishing with large beads

Choose beads that have a large enough hole to fit over the braid. If the fit is good the bead will sit in position on its own, but a little glue applied to the cord will secure it more permanently.

Using a bead as an end cap

1 Wrap the end of the braid with sewing thread (see Finishing Techniques), then stick a large-hole bead over the end of the braid to neaten the end. This technique is suitable for a bell pull or to finish a lariat necklace.

2 You could add a plain or wrapped loop (see General Techniques) so that the large bead replaces an end cap or cone. Allow the glue to dry for 24 hours.

Joining ends in a Y-shape

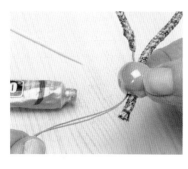

1 Wrap the braids together, then choose a large-hole bead to fit over the ends and cover the wrapping. Apply a little glue over the wrapping, then slide the bead on top to hide the raw ends.

2 To make a tassel, leave the thread ends on the braid. Adding another bundle of threads thickens the tassel and prevents the bead falling off.

Joining ends in a circle

1 Wrap both ends of the braid with strong sewing thread to secure (see Finishing Techniques) and trim neatly. Add a suitable large bead onto the braid.

2 Butt the two ends together and sew long stitches through the wrapping all the way round. Sew in the ends and trim.

3 Apply a little glue over the wrapping and finishing stitches, then slide the bead over so that all the stitching is hidden. Leave to dry.

A pendant slide could be added onto the braid before joining the two ends. This tubular finding has a loop for attaching a charm or bead dangle. Large beads on either side will hide the rest of the join if the finding isn't wide enough.

Finishing with small beads

Seed beads, bugle beads, tiny pearls and crystal bicones are just some of the small bead options for covering joins or to finish ends on Kumihimo braids.

* Join the braid as Joining Ends in a Circle and then stitch groups of small beads lengthways across the stitched join. Add the same number of beads each time to create a little tubular 'beaded bead' to embellish the cord.

* A spiral bead also covers the join. Wrap 0.4mm (27swg) wire around the braid several times, pick up seed beads on the wire and continue to wrap to make the beaded bead, then finish with a few wraps in plain wire.

Finishing with tubular bead stitches

For an ornate finish use one of the tubular bead stitches to cover the join. One of the simplest is the Dutch spiral.

Dutch spiral

The length of bugle you use will depend on the diameter of the braid, or you could add more pairs of seed bead and bugle to fit around the braid. The stitch is illustrated without braid but you should join the braid (see Finishing with small beads) and then tie the beads around the braid ready to start.

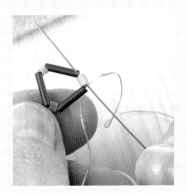

1 Pick up a seed bead then a bugle and repeat twice. Wrap the beads around the braid and then pass the needle through all the beads again to make a circle, coming out after the first seed bead.

2 * Pick up one seed bead and one bugle and pass the needle through the next seed bead. Pull the thread through. Repeat from * circling around the braid, till the tubular bead stitching is long enough to cover the join.

> Closely packed tubular bead stitches such as herringbone stitch, peyote stitch and brick stitch are all suitable.

Slide the beading over the join and sew through the braid to secure, sewing half-hitches into the beading to secure the tail before trimming.

PROJECTS

Throughout this book there are inspiring mini projects that can be made as a quick and easy follow-on to the various techniques and these need no further instruction. Alongside are some fabulous designs to showcase my favourite techniques; these are a little more involved so detailed step-by-step instructions are supplied for you to follow, illustrated with photo details. You should refer back to the knotting and braiding techniques as necessary.

A selection of the mini projects

Knotting

Double coin knot cuff

Double coin knots are usually tied in exactly the same way, one after the other, but the knots lie flatter if the start of the knot is reversed, beginning on the left, then the right, and so on. This creates an attractive pattern with long strands looping across between the double coin knots alternating at the top and bottom edges of the cuff.

You will need

* 9m (10yd) of 2mm leather cord
* Magnetic fastening with 3 x 9mm internal dimension end caps

1 Cut the leather cord into three equal pieces, 3m (3⅓yd) long. Referring to Chinese Knots: Double Coin Knot, tie a double coin knot using all three strands starting with a clockwise loop in your left hand and bringing the working end (right-hand tail) down over the loop. Complete the knot and firm it up so that the top loop is fairly large and all three strands are flat and aligned neatly (see photo below).

2 Make a second double coin knot, this time starting with a loop in your right hand, bringing the working end (left-hand tail) down across the loop, around the other tail, and doubling back to create the second knot..

3 Firm up the second knot, adjusting the position so that it is fairly close but not overlapping the previous knot. Make sure that none of the cords are twisted and that all are lying flat within the knot (see photo below).

> You always know which side to make the loop as you use the tail that is coming from behind the previous knot.

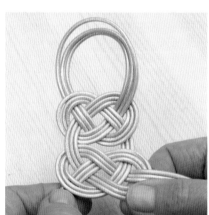

4 Continue tying double coin knots one after the other, swapping the start position from side to side each time.

5 Once you have made six knots, check the length of the cuff. Allowing for the fastening, adjust the distance between each knot if required. Overlap the cords to make a cross after the final knot. Depending on the style of your end cap, either wrap the cords together or sew across to keep the

cord flat (see Finishing Techniques). Trim the ends and stick into the end caps using epoxy resin adhesive. (see photo below).

Prosperity knot belt

The prosperity knot is a large flat knot in the shape of a rectangle, which makes it perfect for making into a belt. You can tie just prosperity knots one after the other, but adding a double coin knot in between keeps the belt flatter, allowing you to adjust it to a more accurate length with the buckle. To embellish, you could add beads between the knots or hang charms from one or two of the loops.

You will need

★ 8.5m (9yd) of 2mm wax cotton cord
★ 12mm (½in) wide buckle
★ Small piece of leather
★ E6000 jewellery glue

1 Fold the cord in half to find the centre and tie a double coin knot in the centre, starting with a loop in the left hand. Referring to Chinese Knots: Prosperity Knot, continue to tie a slightly loose prosperity knot. Firm up by pushing all the overlapping cords up, one at a time, towards the top of the knot, until there are two loops left at the bottom.

2 Pull the top left cord through to pull up the bottom loop on one side. Repeat with the other side. Then pull the tails one at a time to firm up the knot.

3 Repeat the firming up process if necessary to create a closely woven prosperity knot that is about 12mm (½in) wide. Hold the knot firmly between fingers and thumbs in two hands and agitate slightly to align the cords in a more even woven pattern.

4 Tie a double coin knot with the tails, starting with a loop in the right hand this time. Once the knot is tied adjust the position so that it is close to the prosperity knot but not overlapping it. Firm up carefully as you will not be able to adjust it later.

5 Continue to tie alternate prosperity and double coin knots. Remember to alternate the side the start loop is on – left-hand loop for the prosperity knot and right-hand loop for the double coin knot.

6 Once the belt is the length required allowing for overlap, stop after tying a prosperity knot. Loop the ends around the belt buckle twice on each side to fill the gap, and sew securely on the reverse.

7 To make the belt loop, cut a 1 x 3cm (³/8 x 1¹/8in) strip of leather. Apply glue to one end of the leather strip and stick over the stitched cord ends below the buckle. Wrap the strip around the belt so that it overlaps on the reverse side, leaving a loop large enough for the other end of the belt to go through. Apply glue on the overlapping strip and hold in place until the glue dries. Leave for 24 hours before use.

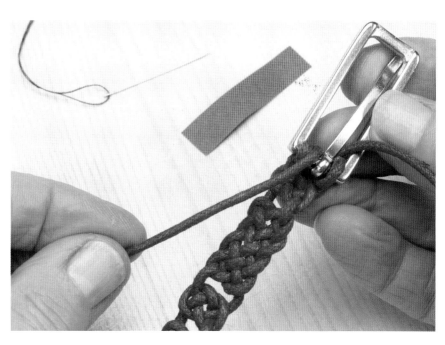

Snake knot tie backs

These instructions are for a tie back measuring about 40cm (16in) long, but the length can be easily adjusted: allow 1.25m (50in) of elastic cord for every 10cm (4in) of finished braid. You can leave the braid plain or embellish it with beads. As the elastic cord is very firm and difficult to stitch through, it is much easier to use a tapestry needle to create a pathway for the finer needle when adding the beads.

You will need

* 5m (5½yd) of 3mm teal elastic cord
* Swarovski Elements: XILION beads 5328, 4mm pacific opal and chrysolite opal, 54 each
* Seed beads size 11 (2.2mm) blue marbled aqua and silver-lined crystal
* Nylon beading thread
* Size 10 beading needle
* Tapestry needle
* Two end caps with 3 x 9mm internal dimension
* Epoxy resin adhesive

1 Cut a 45cm (18in) length of elastic cord, then cut the remaining cord length in two pieces. Referring to Knotted Braids: Snake Knot, work your snake knot braid.

2 Tie a knot in the end of a length of nylon (or matching colour) beading thread and thread a size 10 beading needle. Bend the braid about 5cm (2in) from the end so that you can see the cord pattern between the loops at one side. Insert the tapestry needle between the two straight lengths of braid that you can see.

> It is always more secure to work with a double length of thread when sewing beads onto braid.

3 Push the tapestry needle through the braid to come out between the loops on the other side. Leave the tapestry needle in place; this is the path that the finer threaded needle will take through the braid.

4 Secure the nylon thread between the two side loops above the tapestry needle. Pick up an aqua seed bead, a pacific opal XILION, an aqua seed bead, a silver-lined seed bead, a chrysolite opal XILION, a silver-lined seed bead, an aqua seed bead, a pacific opal XILION, and an aqua seed bead.

5 Lay the beads at an angle across the braid, then take the beading needle back through beside the tapestry needle. Pull both needles through at the same time.

6 Pull the thread taut to secure the beads across the braid. Insert the tapestry needle through the braid again between the next loops, in preparation to add another line of beads. This time reverse the order of the XILIONS, adding two chrysolite and one pacific opal.

7 Repeat to add lines of beads, stopping about 5cm (2in) from the end of the braid. Sew in the thread ends securely.

8 Trim the cord ends to the same length, leaving tails about 2cm (¾in) long. Mix a little epoxy resin adhesive and use a cocktail stick to apply inside one end cap. Push two of the cord ends into the end cap and use a cocktail stick (or awl) to push the remaining cord in place. Repeat to attach an end cap at the other end, and leave to dry.

> To give the finished tieback maximum impact buy (or make) more braid cords in toning colours, cutting them so that some are slightly shorter than the snake knot rope and others slightly longer. Finish with whipped loops at each end and secure around the curtain with ribbon.

Switchback bracelet

This bracelet is not a set pattern and can be made with your own combination of different knotting techniques. Work approximately 51cm (20in) so that it wraps around your wrist three times, and check the positioning of the beads on the bracelet as you go as they should be on the top of your wrist rather than below.

You will need

* ✶ 1.25m (1½yd) of 1mm off-white pearlized leather cord
* ✶ 3m (3¼yd) each of 1mm and 1.5mm brown wax cotton cord
* ✶ 5m (5½yd) of cream Superlon™ Tex 400 (0.9mm)
* ✶ Swarovski Elements: Square Mini-beads, eight 6mm light silk
* ✶ Double delica (size 8) seed beads, approx 50 dark topaz rainbow 103
* ✶ Metal button
* ✶ E6000 jewellery glue or epoxy resin adhesive
* ✶ Pin board and map pins (optional)

1 Fold the leather cord in half. To prevent the pearlized leather getting damaged, loop a short piece of scrap cord around it using a lark's head knot and secure to a pin board or work surface.

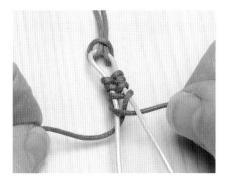

2 Using the 1.5mm wax cotton cord and referring to Switchback Braids: Single Cord Switchback Braid, begin to work an 8cm (3in) length of regular switchback braid over the leather cord. After about 2.5cm (1in) adjust the size of the loop to suit the button you are using for the bracelet and then continue.

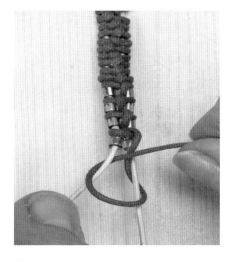

3 Pick up 14 double delicas on each end of the leather cord. Drop one of the tails of the wax cotton cord and work stitched switchback (see Switchback Braids: Stitched Switchback Strap) pushing beads up between the knots, securing them in place as you tie the next knot.

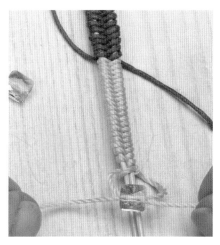

4 Change to the cream Superlon™ Tex and work an 8cm (3in) length of regular switchback. Work the first half of a macramé square knot (see Macramé: Macramé Knots). Pick up

a square mini-bead on one cord and feed the other tail through the hole in the opposite direction.

> Melt the end of the cord with a lighter flame and trim to make it easier to feed it through the bead.

5 Tie a square knot around both leather cords so that the bead is sitting flat. Add seven more mini-beads, tying a square knot after each one. Work another 2.5cm (1in) of switchback in cream.

6 Continue to work the second half of the bracelet, using different thicknesses of cord, changing from regular switchback to stitched switchback, incorporating double delica beads or working a length without beads as you choose. Finish with a length of regular switchback worked with the 1mm wax cord.

7 Check the length, then tie the button onto the end of the leather cords; trim the leather and stick to the reverse side of the button using epoxy resin or E6000 jewellery glue.

Rhinestone bracelets

Micro macramé worked with a fine knotting cord is perfect for making delicate jewellery. Seed beads can be added to the outer cords to make a simple beaded bracelet or add a little bling by knotting the cords around rhinestone cup chain.

You will need

★ 11cm (4¼in) of 4mm (stretched out) rhinestone cup chain
★ 2.5m (2¾yd) of 1mm nylon knotting cord
★ E6000 jewellery glue
★ Pin board and map pins (optional)

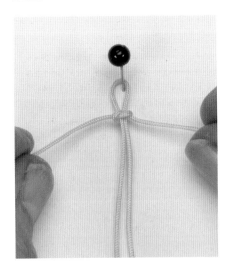

1 Cut a 50cm (20in) length from the knotting cord, and fold both pieces in half. Pin or tape the short length to the work surface with the loop at the top. Tie the longer piece of cord around the short length with an overhand knot.

> Flip the overhand knot to the reverse side after you have tied it to make a neater transition to the macramé.

2 For a 17.5cm (7in) long bracelet, work 3cm (1⅛in) of square knots (see Macramé Basics: Macramé Knots). Insert a pin or tape at the bottom of the knots to hold them in place.

3 Lay the length of cup chain on top of the two cord threads. Work a square knot between each rhinestone on the cup chain (see Adding Beads to Macramé: Adding Rhinestones). Look to see where the bar is on top of the previous square knot: if it is on the right, then begin the next square square knot with the right cord; if it is on the left, start with the left cord. Continue working a square knot between every rhinestone, alternating the side you begin the knot to keep the square knots balanced.

4 Finish the macramé with a 3cm (1⅛in) section of square knots or work the length to match the other end. Check the length of the bracelet and adjust if necessary. Work a two-strand button knot over two cords, weaving the cords in pairs (see Chinese Knots: Button Knot). Tighten the button knot gradually, pulling the cords through so that it is sitting about 3–5mm (⅛–¼in) from the square knots (see photo above).

5 Apply a little glue inside the button knot where the cords emerge at the base, and trim the cords once the glue has dried. Check that the loop at the other end of the bracelet goes over the button knot snugly. You can adjust slightly by pulling the macramé knots down or up the centre core cords. Apply a little glue on the reverse side to secure the loop at the correct size.

Beaded macramé bracelet

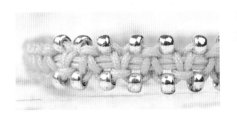

Begin the bracelet in exactly the same way as the rhinestone bracelet, and instead of adding the cup chain in the centre section, pick up a size 6 (3.5mm) seed bead on each outer cord and tie the next square knot (see Adding Beads to Macramé: Adding Beads to Working Cords). You will need 20 seed beads for a 17.5cm (7in) bracelet.

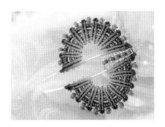

Macramé brooch

Macramé is often thought of as a rather crude chunky knotting technique, but when worked in fine cords it transforms into rather elegant micro macramé. Choose coordinating colours to create a rainbow effect across this pretty brooch.

You will need

* ✷ 1.5m (1¾yd) each of Superlon™ cord in purple, lilac, coral, light grey and dusky pink
* ✷ 20cm (8in) of 1mm (19swg) half hard sterling silver wire
* ✷ Seed beads: size 6 (3.5mm) matte silver, size 10 (2mm) colour-lined peach, size 11 (2.2mm) silver-lined crystal and emerald raspberry gold lustre
* ✷ Ultrasuede™ 10cm (4in) square
* ✷ Brooch back
* ✷ Jewellery tools
* ✷ Chasing hammer and steel block (optional)
* ✷ Foam core board
* ✷ Map pins
* ✷ Adhesive tape
* ✷ Spring clip (optional)

1 Bend the silver wire in half to create a slightly round ended 'V' shape. Arrange the Superlon™ cords in order ready to use: purple, lilac, coral, light grey and dusky pink.

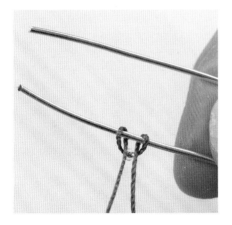

2 Pick up a silver-lined crystal seed bead on the purple cord and drop to the centre. Fold the cord in half and lay it over the wire on one side of the 'V'.

Take the tails over the wire and back through the loop to make a reverse lark's head knot (Knotting Basics: Basic Knots)

3 Work a half-hitch on either side (see Macramé Basics: Macramé Knots). Repeat steps 2 and 3 with the other coloured cords, adding a bead each time.

4 Lay the wire shape on the foam core board and tape in position. *Bring the end purple cord across parallel to the wire. Work a double half-hitch with each cord in turn (see Multistrand Macramé: Straight Half-hitch Rib).

5 Insert a map pin at the end of the rib, then take the purple cord back across the vertical cords at a slight angle. Secure with tape or a spring

clip. Work double half-hitches with the dusky pink cords and the first grey cord. Pick up a colour-lined peach seed bead on the next grey cord and work double half-hitches again.

> The beads added on the vertical cords will determine the angle of the half-hitch rib.

6 Work double half-hitches with the first coral cord, then pick up two silver-lined crystal seed beads on the next coral cord; secure with double half-hitches. Add three emerald raspberry gold lustre seed beads on the first lilac cord, securing with double half-hitches again.

7 Work double half-hitches on the next lilac cord before finishing with a silver-lined crystal, a size 6 matte silver and a silver-lined crystal on the remaining purple cord. Work the last double half-hitch.

continued overleaf

10 Repeat on the two grey cords and then work down the wire, adding beads on the first of each colour, reducing the number of silver-lined beads as the gap between the wires narrows.

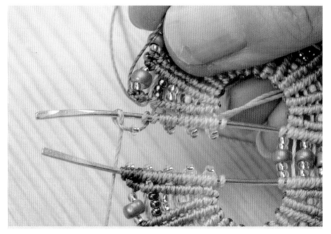

8 Repeat from * six or seven times, depending on your tension, until the semicircle of macramé curves around to meet the wire again. Take the purple cord back to the outside edge again, working straight half-hitch rib. Work double half-hitches with each cord in turn over the wire.

11 Work a semicircle in macramé to match the first side, ending with a straight half-hitch rib. Work a double half-hitch with the first cord and add a silver-lined crystal. Work another double half-hitch with the same cord to secure the bead. Repeat with every second cord.

12 Fold the cord ends over the back of the macramé and stitch invisibly with tiny stitches. Trim neatly. Cut Ultrasuede™ to fit each semicircle and stitch in place invisibly around the edge.

9 Tuck all the cord tails behind the silver wire. Pick up two silver-lined crystals, a size 6 matte silver seed bead and two silver-lined crystals on the first dusky pink cord. Work a double half-hitch on the other side of the wire 'V' shape. Attach the next dusky pink cord without beads.

13 Sew a brooch back to one side on the reverse of the brooch, stitching right through to the right side, then coming back through to the reverse so that the tiny stitch is hidden between the macramé knots. Sew the ends in securely.

Braiding

Plaited silk and pearl necklace

Three-strand plaiting is one of the simplest braiding techniques, and because of its simplicity you can braid quite chunky strands together incorporating an eclectic mix of materials. Silk organza and delicate pearls make an elegant necklace for evening, or choose a fun fabric with bright beads for a summer's day.

You will need

* Silk organza, 50 x 30cm (20 x 12in) pale pink
* Pearls, approx 200 4mm dusty pink
* 1.3m (49in) each of chain in gold, antique gold and bronze
* 3m (3¼yd) of 8mm (5/16in) Kojaku ribbon in Strasborg Canal
* 3m (3¼yd) each of 5mm (¼in) Isuki ribbon in manila and soft pink
* 1m (39in) of 19 strand 0.38mm (0.015in) bead stringing wire
* Fine 0.315mm (30swg) wire
* Two eyepins antique gold-plated
* Two end caps antique gold-plated with 10mm internal diameter
* Pale pink sewing thread
* Needles: sewing and large tapestry
* Lobster claw fastening 12mm antique gold
* Jump ring 6mm antique gold
* Small bead springs or tape
* Jewellery tools
* E6000 jewellery glue

1 Cut the silk organza into three 10cm (4in) wide strips. Fold each in half lengthways and sew down the centre with running stitch. Sew in the thread ends securely and leave long tails. Use a rouleau loop turning tool to hook one end and pull the fabric tube inside out. You could also use a tapestry needle tied to the thread tails to pull the fabric

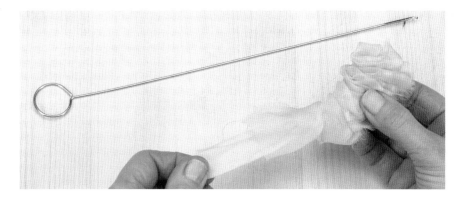

tube through to the right side. Repeat to turn the other two tubes inside out (see photo above).

2 Use a cool iron to press the silk tubes with the seam on one edge and lay them side by side on the work surface. Cut the ribbons into 50cm (20in) lengths. Lay two lengths of each of the ribbon on top of each of the silk tubes.

3 Cut the bead stringing wire in half. Attach a narrow strip of tape or bead spring 5cm (2in) from the end. Pick up half the pearls on each string and secure with tape or a bead spring. Lay bead strings on top of two of the silk tubes (see photo below). Wrap the three tubes together with the fine wire so that ribbons and pearls are lying on top of the silk tubes.

4 Cut the chains in half and feed the fine wire into the end links. Wrap wire a few times to secure. Lay two chains on top of each of the three bundles. Secure the wired end of the prepared bundles to the work surface with tape or a spring clip. Plait the bundles keeping the tubes of fabric fairly flat with the chain, pearls and ribbon on the top surface (see Plaiting: Three-strnd Plaiting).

5 Plait about 35cm (14in) to the end of the pearls, then secure the plait again, wrapping the silk, pearl string and

ribbons with fine wire. Trim the chains so that they are level with the wrapped wire and secure by threading the wire through the end links only so that they will sit below the end cap. Wrap wire around a few more times.

6 Trim the excess fabric and ribbons above the wrapped wire so that the raw ends will fit inside the end cap. Glue an end cap over each end of the plait to cover the wires and raw edges and leave to dry. Attach about 13cm (5in) of chain to each end. Finish with a jump ring and lobster claw fastening.

Chain plait necklace

This beautiful necklace makes a real statement but is actually quite easy to create. The base is made by plaiting embroidery cotton and ribbon into chunky chain, then headpin dangles are attached. The finished design is then draped with fine chain.

You will need

* Antique copper chain: 30cm (12in) with 15 x 12mm links, 1m (39in) with 3 x 4mm links, and 20cm (8in) with 6 x 5mm links
* DMC cotton perlé: one skein each of plum and orange
* 50cm (18in) each of 1cm (³⁄₈in) organza ribbon in lilac and pale orange
* 1.5m (1¾yd) of fine chain gold-plated chain with 3 x 2mm links
* 40cm (16in) of tubular wire mesh in burgundy

* Swarovski Elements:
  Large Dome beads 5541, three 15mm crystal lilac shadow
  Small Dome beads 5542, two 8mm crystal lilac shadow
  Round Crystal beads 5000, four 8mm crystal lilac shadow, 21 4mm crystal copper
  Round Crystal pearls 5818, two 8mm, three 6mm and four 4mm blackberry
  Drop Crystal pearls 5816, two 11.5 x 6mm blackberry
  Coin Crystal pearls 5860, five 14mm blackberry

* 14 ball end headpins 4cm antique copper
* Fine wire for wrapping
* Two end caps antique copper with 8mm internal diameter
* E6000 jewellery glue or epoxy resin adhesive
* Jewellery tools
* Lobster claw fastening 9mm antique copper
* Jump rings antique copper: two 4mm and one 6mm

1 Open out the skeins of cotton perlé then cut through each of the bundles at the knot. Lay a length of matching organza ribbon on top of each of the embroidery skeins.

2 Secure the two bundles with an overhand knot. On the orange, lay a length of the fine gold-plated chain cut to size, and on the plum lay the length of metal mesh. Plait the bundles into the chain with the largest links (see Plaiting with Beads and Chain: Two-strand Plaiting with Chain). Secure the plaiting at each end with fine wire.

3 Trim the end from five headpins. Make a loop on one end of each. Pick up a coin crystal pearl on each loop headpin. Bend the tail over at right angles, trim to 7mm (9/32in) and make a loop on the end (see General Techniques: Making a Plain Loop).

4 Attach one coin crystal blackberry pearl bead link to the centre of the plaited chain. Working to either side of this centre bead link, miss three links, then attach another coin crystal blackberry pearl bead, and repeat to

add the remaining two bead links. To make the large dangles, pick up a 6mm round crystal blackberry pearl, a large dome bead and a 4mm round crystal copper bead. Make a loop on the end. Attach to the central coin bead link. Make two other dangles the same and attach to the coin bead link at either side.

5 To make the smaller bead dangles in the same style, use a 4mm round crystal pearl, small dome bead and a 4mm round crystal copper bead. Attach to the outer coin bead links.

6 Pick up an 8mm crystal blackberry pearl, 8mm round crystal lilac shadow bead, a 4mm round blackberry pearl and a 4mm crystal copper bead. Make into a dangle with a loop and attach to the middle link between the two outer coin bead links on each side of the necklace.

7 Trim the end off two headpins, and use E6000 jewellery glue to stick a blackberry drop crystal pearl onto each. Once dry pick up a 4mm crystal copper bead, an 8mm crystal lilac shadow bead, a 4mm round blackberry pearl and a 4mm crystal copper bead. Make a loop on the end and attach to the middle chain link at either side of the centre dangle.

8 Secure the rest of the fine gold chain to one end of the plaiting by wrapping with more fine wire. Drape the chain around the necklace, using a bodkin to feed the wire through the plait on the reverse side.from

time to time to secure. Repeat with the antique copper chain with 3 x 4mm links, and then trim and secure both lengths to the other end of the plait with fine wire. Sew the remaining crystal copper round beads into the front of the plait randomly.

9 Trim the plait above the wrapped wire and then attach an end cap to each end with strong glue such as E6000 or epoxy resin (see Finishing Techniques). Attach a 10cm (4in) length of the antique copper chain with 6 x 5mm links to each end cap. Check the length and trim the chain if required. Attach a lobster claw fastening to one end of the chain with a small jump ring and use a small jump ring to attach a larger jump ring to complete the fastening at the other end.

Round braid earrings

Embellished with Swarovski Elements including beautiful Baroque pendants, these elegant earrings are easy to make. Superlon™, a stiff nylon cord, is used to make a fine firm braid, then the earrings are finished with high-quality end caps designed especially for two 4–5mm cords.

You will need

* 1m (39in) each of Superlon™ cord in deep pink, dark grey, steel grey and teal
* Sewing thread and needle
* Swarovski Elements:
  Baroque pendant 6090, two 16mm ruby
  XILION beads 5328, two 6mm ruby, two 6mm pacific opal
  Crystal pearl 5810, two 6mm Tahitian-look
* Two Silversilk Capture double-strand end cap gunmetal with 8 x 9mm internal dimensions
* Two headpins gunmetal
* Two jump rings gunmetal
* Two triangle bails gunmetal
* Two earring wires gunmetal
* Kumihimo disk
* Weight approx 100g (4oz)
* Sewing thread
* Jewellery tools
* Nylon-jaw pliers

1 Prepare the Superlon™ threads by pressing lightly with a medium steam iron to straighten out the curves and make the thread more supple. Fold the bundle of cords in half and set up the disk (see Kumihimo: Preparing to Braid), arranging the cords in the starting position shown in the diagram.

Starting position

2 Referring to Round Braids: Round Braid 2, work a 20cm (8in) length. Remove the braid from the disk and wrap near the end with sewing thread. Measure 8cm (3in) and wrap again. Leave a small gap, then wrap with thread one more time, before measuring a second 8cm (3in) length. Cut the braid into two pieces close to the wrapping (see also Finishing Techniques: Wrapping).

3 Take one of the round braid pieces and insert the ends into one of the end caps, squeezing with nylon-jaw pliers to close to secure the braid ends in place. Repeat to make the other earring.

4 Attach a triangle bail to each Baroque pendant bead, then attach a jump ring (see General Techniques: Adding a Jump Ring). Tuck the jump ring between the ends of the braid and stitch in place with tiny stitches so that it is secured invisibly as shown above.

5 To make the bead dangles, pick up a ruby XILION bead, a crystal pearl, and a pacific opal XILION bead onto a headpin. Make a large loop (see General Techniques: Making a Plain Loop), and thread onto one of the short braid lengths. Repeat for the second earring.

6 To finish each earring, open the loop on an earring wire and attach to the loop on the end cap.

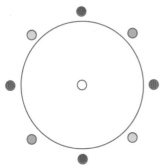

Square braid necklace

Square braid has a more distinctive flat-sided structure when worked in leather and produces a firm braid that can be shaped to fit around the neck. The braid is finished with attractive end caps that become part of the design of the necklace. Worked here in gold the design would look equally good in silver or gunmetal.

You will need

* 8m (8¾yd) of 1.5mm pearlized ivory leather cord
* Four end caps gold-plated with 8mm internal diameter
* Swarovski Elements:
  Round Crystal pearls 5810, nine 8mm and one 4mm night blue
  Artemis bead 5540, one 17mm crystal golden shadow
* 0.6mm (24swg) gold-plated wire
* Headpin gold-plated
* Three jump rings gold-plated
* Barrel fastening gold-plated
* Kumihimo plate
* Weight approx 100g (4oz)
* Fine wire
* Jewellery tools
* E6000 jewellery glue

1 Cut the leather cord into four equal pieces and attach with a lark's head loop in the middle. Referring to Kumihimo: Round Braids: Square Braid, set up the disk and work a 36cm (14in) length of square braid.

2 Remove the braid from the disk and secure the loose end with a wrapping of fine wire. Measure 15cm (6in) and wrap the braid with fine wire. Leave

a small gap then wrap the braid with wire again. Measure another 15cm (6in), then wrap with wire one last time. Cut the braid into two pieces close to the wire wrapping.

3 Glue an end cap onto each end of the two pieces of square braid; leave to dry (see Finishing Techniques).

4 Make eight of the 8mm crystal pearls into individual bead links using the 0.6mm (24swg) wire (see General Techniques: Making a Plain Loop). Join the bead links together in two groups of four.

5 Attach one length of the bead links onto each length of square braid. The pearl bead link lengths will be joined together with a jump ring, but first make the centre Artemis bead dangle. Pick up the remaining 8mm crystal pearl on the headpin, then the Artemis bead and the crystal 4mm pearl. Fold over the headpin at the top, trim to 7mm (⁹/₃₂in), and make a plain loop.

6 Open the top of the Artemis bead dangle, and attach with a jump ring in the middle of the pearl bead link lengths. Use a jump ring to attach the fastening to the end caps at the end of the square braid sections.

Stacking beaded bracelets

Several narrow bracelets worn together in a stack are one of the most popular trends in jewellery and the perfect way to show off this pretty design, which is a variation of the rounded flat braid worked in thick and thin cords with the beads added on the thin cords. So long as the thin strands are placed where shown in the starting position diagram, you can try all sorts of colour variations to make a matching set of stacking bracelets. The materials listed are sufficient to make one bracelet, measuring 17cm (6¾in) long.

You will need

* ✷ 2m (2⅛yd) of 2mm silver grey rattail
* ✷ 1m (39in) each of Superlon™ cord in purple and teal
* ✷ Seed beads size 8 (3mm), 16 each of purple iris and silver gloss
* ✷ Kumihimo square plate
* ✷ Weight approx 100g (4oz)
* ✷ Magnetic or lobster claw fastening
* ✷ Ribbon crimp 6mm
* ✷ Two jump rings 4mm
* ✷ E6000 jewellery glue

1 Lay the cords side by side and loop the scrap of fine cord around the middle using a lark's head knot. Set up the cords in the square plate ready to work the rounded flat braid (see Kumihimo: Flat Braids: Using a Square Plate to Make a Rounded Flat Braid). To get this exact pattern arrange the cords as shown in the diagram.

Starting position

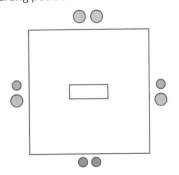

It is especially important with a flat braid to keep the cords in the correct slots so that the braid is even and the threads sit at the correct angle.

2 Pick up eight purple iris seed beads on each of the purple Superlon™ strands and eight silver gloss seed beads on the teal Superlon™ strands, tying a knot at the end of the strands to stop the beads falling off.

3 Work the rounded flat braid keeping the fine yarns slightly loose so that they show as a 'V' shape on the front of the braid. Work 6cm (2⅜in) of rounded flat braid without beads finishing at the end of the four-pair sequence of moves so that the cords are back in the original position.

4 Begin to incorporate the beads during the next sequence. When the fine cords are being moved from the side position to the bottom (from E to 15 and e to 16), add a bead on each side, allowing the beads to fall down to the work so that each bead is tucked under the other colour of Superlon™ cord currently in the d and D slots. You'll add beads on the purple cord on one four-pair sequence and on the teal cord in the next (see photo above).

5 Once you have added all the beads, continue working the unembellished rounded flat braid for another 6cm (2⅜in). Remove the cords from the slots, wrap one of the Superlon™ cords around the bottom of the braid and tie a reef knot to secure.

6 Check the length of the bracelet including the fastening. Referring to Finishing Techniques: Finishing with Cord Ends, End Caps and Cones, attach the ribbon crimps to the ends of the braid: secure the ends by stitching, trim neatly, and stick in place with E6000 jewellery glue. Leave to dry for 24 hours before attaching the fastening to each end with a jump ring.

Kumihimo hollow braid brooch

Wire Kumihimo braid is phenomenally tactile and easily manipulated. A bit of experimenting with the flattened wire braid created this fabulous Celtic knot shape that evolved into a stunning brooch. The design would also work as a hair decoration.

You will need

* 50g reels of 0.315mm (30swg) wire in steel grey and champagne
* Swarovski Elements:
  Solaris Fancy Stones 4678, one 23mm crystal silver night, one 14mm crystal luminous green and three 8mm dark moss green
  Solaris Fancy stone settings 4678/G, one 23mm, one 14mm, and three 8mm
  XILION beads 5328, eight each in 3mm light silk: jonquil, olivine, and black diamond
* Kumihimo disk
* Weight approx 100g (4oz)
* Brooch back
* Fine wire
* Beading needle
* Jewellery tools

Starting position

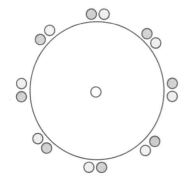

1 Using pegs secured 50cm (20in) apart on the bench, wind each colour of wire around 16 times (see Kumihimo: Working with Wire: Preparing the Wire). Separate into groups of four and then cut into lengths. Set up the disk for 16-strand hollow braid (Kumihimo: Hollow Braids): you don't need a core as the wire will hold the round shape as you work. Arrange the coloured wires in groups of four and alternate the colours all the way round.

> A weight of around 100–150g (4–6oz) will help to keep the weaving even along the length.

2 Work the braid as described in Kumihimo: Hollow Braids: 16-strand Hollow Braid. After you work clockwise with one colour and then anticlockwise with the other, give the weight a tug to pull the braid down through the hole in the middle of the disk (see photo below).

3 Continue to work the braid. The nature of the weaving technique will mean that the wires should lie side by side as you work to create an even flat braid. From time to time check the positioning of the wires and rearrange side by side so that the braid is as even as possible.

4 Once the braid is complete, remove it from the disk and flatten. Remove the lark's head loop from the end of the braid. Hold the braid and push in towards the middle to create a wider section (see photo below).

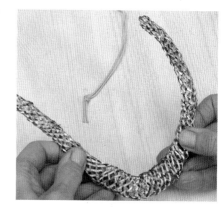

5 Tie the ends of the braid in an overhand knot shape, overlapping the start end over the bottom edge of the wire shape. Arrange the wire braid into an attractive Celtic knot shape and fold the braid end over the edge to secure.

6 Shape the widest part of the brooch shape over your fingers so that it has a curved cross-section. Set the fancy stones into their settings: lay the stones on top of the setting so that it is level, then use snipe-nose pliers to bend each of the lugs over the stone in turn.

9 Sew the remaining fancy stones on the top of the brooch. Pick up a selection of XILION beads and arrange on a fine wire around the curve of the largest fancy stone and couch down by oversewing across the wire and between the XILION beads. Sew more XILION beads around the edge of the hole.

7 The largest fancy stone has a deep setting so you need to make a 'dip' for it to rest in so that it is not raised on the finished design. Fold the loose end of the wire braid at right angles as it crosses the hole in the brooch. Fold across the hole allowing for the depth of the setting, then fold back up at the other side of the hole.

8 Secure the wire braid on the reverse side of the brooch by stitching with fine wire, and trim the excess. Set the largest fancy stone into the gap so that the holes in the side of the setting are level with the braid. Sew in place with fine wire.

10 Stitch a brooch fitment onto the reverse of the brooch, to the braid that runs beneath the largest fancy stone. Check the shaping, curving the wire mesh smoothly over your fingers so that the brooch back is inset rather than standing proud beyond the level of the back of the brooch.

SUPPLIERS

The companies listed all had Kumihimo and knotting supplies at the time of printing. Check the websites for particular cords and findings as stocks change from time to time.

UK and Europe

Beads Direct
Tel: 01509 218028
Email: service@beadsdirect.co.uk
Web: www.beadsdirect.co.uk

Bead Workshop
Tel: 01333 424400
Email: support@beadworkshop.co.uk
Web: www.bead-workshop.co.uk

Carey Company
Tel: 01404 813486
Email: carey@ careycompany.com
Web: www.careycompany.com

Heavenly Beads
Tel: 01324 228353
Email: heavenlybeads@hotmail.co.uk
Web: www.heavenlybeads.co.uk

I-Beads
Tel: 0207 367 6217
Email: info@i-beads.co.uk
Web: www.i-beads.co.uk
FR: www.i-perles.fr
DE: www.i-perlen.de
AT: www.i-perlen.at

Nosek's Just Gems
Tel: 01225 706222
Email: caron@noseks.co.uk
Web: www.noseksjustgems.com

Stitch Craft Create
Web: www.stitchcraftcreate.co.uk

The London Bead Company
Tel: 0207 267 9403
Email: orders@londonbead.co.uk
Web: www.londonbead.co.uk

USA

Accent Bead Design
Tel: 916 9411104
Email: support@accentbead.com
Web: www.accentbead.com

The Bead Shop
Tel: 650 3866962
Email: info@beadshop.com
Web: www.beadshop.com

The Satin Cord Store
Tel: 888 7288245
Email: cathy@satincord.com
Web: www.satin cords.com

Acknowledgments

I've thoroughly enjoyed writing this new bible, focussing on knotting and braiding techniques. My two previous bibles, *The Beader's Bible* and *The Bead Jewellery Bible*, have been a huge success and I hope that this new book encourages lots of people to try out some fabulous new techniques. It was a new challenge researching the different knots and braids and I would like to thank two friends, Carole Cowie and Shelagh Fraser, for their help making some of the braid samples and small projects. Thanks to all suppliers for their generosity supplying materials used in the book. All books require a background team and this is no exception. I'd particularly like to thank Jeni Hennah for commissioning the book, editor Sarah Callard for keeping me on track and Charly Bailey for a fantastic book design. Thanks also to Cheryl Brown for copy editing the manuscript. Finally thanks to Ally Stuart for her skilled step-by-step photography and Jack Kirby for the beautiful finished shots.

TEMPLATES

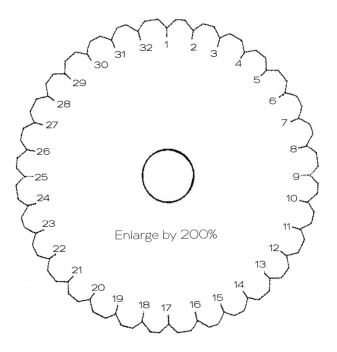

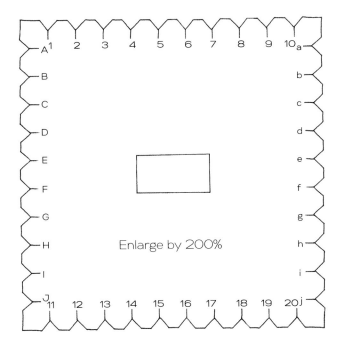

INDEX

A DAVID & CHARLES BOOK
© F&W Media International, Ltd 2014

David & Charles is an imprint of F&W Media International, Ltd
Brunel House, Forde Close, Newton Abbot, TQ12 4PU, UK

F&W Media International, Ltd is a subsidiary of F+W Media, Inc
10151 Carver Road, Suite #200, Blue Ash, OH 45242, USA

Text and Designs © Dorothy Wood 2014
Layout and Photography © F&W Media International, Ltd 2014

First published in the UK and USA in 2014

A catalogue record for this book is available from the British
Library.

ISBN-13: 978-1-4463-0394-8 paperback
ISBN-10: 1-4463-0394-2 paperback

Printed in China by RR Donnelley for:
F&W Media International, Ltd
Brunel House, Forde Close, Newton Abbot, TQ12 4PU, UK
10 9 8 7 6 5 4 3 2 1

Acquisitions Editor: Sarah Callard
Desk Editor: Matthew Hutchings
Project Editor: Cheryl Brown
Art Editor: Charly Bailey
Step photography: Ally Stuart
Project photography: Jack Kirby
Senior Production Controller: Kelly Smith

F+W Media publishes high quality books on a wide
range of subjects.
For more great book ideas visit: www.stitchcraftcreate.co.uk